THE ABERCROMBIE & FITCH LIBRARY

THE DRY FLY & FAST WATER

AND

THE SALMON & THE DRY FLY

George M. L. La Branche

Van Cortlandt
Press

Croton-on-Hudson, N.Y.

A Note to the Reader

In 1951 this combined volume of two American fishing classics by George M. L. La Branche was first published. *The Dry Fly and Fast Water* (1914) and *The Salmon and the Dry Fly* (1924) had been out of print for many years. The combined volume itself is now reprinted for one basic reason: La Branche is required reading for every generation of fishermen.

La Branche is the American angler who conquered the brown trout. The brown trout had been imported from Europe and stocked in eastern trout streams in the late 1880s. Better fitted than the brook trout for survival under modern conditions, the brown trout not only replaced the brook trout which was disappearing from waters made warm by deforestation, but established itself in parts of the streams never hospitable to brook trout.

But it was difficult for brook-trout fishermen to catch the brown trout. The newcomer was more of a surface feeder, more a feeder on insects, and altogether more exacting in its feeding requirements. The answer seemed to be the dry fly, which the British had used for a hundred years or so. However, it developed that the flies and methods used on English chalk streams were largely impractical under American conditions.

George La Branche, out of a long and varied experience with the dry fly on American waters, with a splendidly developed talent for casting and controlling the fly under all sorts of adverse conditions, found the solution. He analyzed the requirements of American fishing and formulated what was in fact a whole new school of dry-fly angling to meet them.

In his introduction to the combined volume, Alfred W. Miller (Sparse Grey Hackle of the The Anglers' Club, a well-known fishing writer and commentator) expresses the opinion that La Branche's works are as valuable and useful to the angler now as when they were written, because they are authoritative and fundamental.

Other experts concur in this opinion.

"La Branche's lessons have endured, not alone because of their incorruptible wisdom, but because of the manner in which they are taught."—Howard T. Walden II, *Angler's Choice*

"The book proves to be written with a very attractive precision and flexibility of style by a man who reveals himself an unusual student of the fine and more delicate arts of fishing. It is, therefore, a book which any sportsman will count as an added prize in his library and which the man who has even a slight interest in fishing will find fascinating."—*Springfield Republican*

"His book is so charmingly written that it will prove most interesting not only to dry-fly fishermen, but to all who love the great outdoors, for it has evidently come from the heart and pen of a nature lover as well as an expert angler."—E. M. Gill, *The New York Times*

C. A. P.

THE DRY FLY AND FAST WATER
AND
THE SALMON AND THE DRY FLY

George M. L. LaBranche,
from the etching by
Gordon Stevenson

The Dry Fly
and
Fast Water

and

The Salmon
and
The Dry Fly

by

GEORGE M. L. LA BRANCHE

CHARLES SCRIBNER'S SONS, NEW YORK
CHARLES SCRIBNER'S SONS, LTD., LONDON
1951

Among the first to apply in practice the principles advanced in "The Dry Fly and Fast Water" and "The Salmon and the Dry Fly" were the members of a small group of ardent and devoted anglers whose companionship I have enjoyed since its formation in 1906. It is a pleasure, therefore, to dedicate this combined edition of the two works to

THE ANGLERS' CLUB OF NEW YORK

INTRODUCTION

In a changing world, angling is one of the least changing of the arts. Over the years, the fish have not changed, nor have the insects. Save in detail, the tackle has not changed, either. And ice and flood have never ceased their annual sculpturing of the rivers. "The Dry Fly and Fast Water" and "The Salmon and the Dry Fly" therefore remain today not only as fascinating but as useful, sound and informative—and as authoritative—as they were when they first appeared.

"The Dry Fly and Fast Water" was written to fill a need created by the coming of the brown trout to America. The British flies and methods which followed it over here proved inapplicable, as the native brook-trout flies and methods proved inadequate to the taking of the newcomer in our water. So it remained for George La Branche to promulgate a new, distinctively American school of dry-fly angling, and the proof of its validity is that today it is universally practised here.

"The Salmon and the Dry Fly" is a memorial to La Branche's dear friend, mentor and fishing colleague, the late Ambrose Monell, and as such reflects but modestly the author's original and outstanding contributions to the new sport of dry-fly fishing for Atlantic salmon which was developed on Col. Monell's water on the Upsalquitch. Although La Branche showed the British that their salmon could be brought to the dry fly, the sport has remained a distinctively American—or at least, North American—one and is thus the second to reflect his mastery of the dry fly.

These two books, long out of print, have been combined in the present volume to meet the insistent demand of those who had read them in the past and wanted to read them again——the best recommendation to the young angler to read them also.

Let him first read them through for his fascination and delight; but then let him study them line by line, for they are compactly written and do not waste words. And if he re-reads them often, he will still find in them each time some new and stimulating thought.

Alfred W. Miller
Sparse Grey Hackle

The Anglers' Club of New York
September 24, 1951.

CONTENTS

THE DRY FLY
AND FAST WATER

PREFACE

To expound a theory into willing ears upon a trout stream is one thing; to put those same ideas into writing so that they may be intelligently conveyed to one who reads them is quite a different thing. Of this I am convinced. However this may be, my readiness to do the one induced in some of my angling friends the belief that I could do the other. They insisted that I try—and this book is the result. My experience in preparing these pages has filled me with the profoundest respect for those persons who may be truthfully characterised as authors. I began the work with a good deal if timidity, and, as it now appears to me, considerable temerity. After completing the task to the best of my ability I submitted the manuscript to some of my credulous friends. Strange to say, after reading it, even then they insisted that I publish it. By this decision it seems to me they proved two things—their friendship for me and their absolute unfitness to be literary critics. Even so, under their instruction and guidance, the book is presented to the angling public with the hope that it may find some small favour among them.

G. M. L. La B.

May, 1914.

CHAPTER I
EARLY EXPERIENCES

ROM my earliest boyhood I have been devoted to the
fly fisher's art, having been inducted into it by my
father, who was an ardent angler before me. For
more than twenty years I have fished the near-by streams
of New York and Pennsylvania; not a season has passed
without having brought to me the pleasure of casting a fly
over their waters. Each recurring year I find myself, as
the season approaches, eagerly looking forward to the
bright days when I can again go upon the streams. In the
early days of the season, however, I am content to over-
haul my gear, to dream alone, or talk with others about the
active days to come; for I have never enjoyed going upon
the waters so long as the air still holds chill winter's bite.

During the early years of my angling I fished my flies
wet or sunk. Such was the manner universally prevailing
upon our streams and the manner of my teaching. I had
read about the dry fly and knew that its use was general
in England, which country may justly be said to be its
place of origin. That this is true may not be gainsaid, yet
it seems to me remarkable that with all the reputed ingenuity of Americans the present development of dry fly fishing
for trout should be almost entirely the work of British

1

sportsmen. That the use of the dry fly on streams in this country has not been more common may be due to a pardonable disinclination upon the part of expert wet fly anglers to admit the weakness of their method under conditions as they now exist. Their method has served them well, as it did their fathers before them, and perhaps they are loath to surrender it for something new. In earlier days trout were much more abundant in our streams, and the men who fished the streams and wrote upon the subject of fly fishing in this country may have felt that a knowledge of the habits and haunts of the fish was more essential to success in taking them than the employment of any particular method. The merits of up-stream over down-stream fishing caused some discussion among anglers, and some of these discussions found permanent place in angling literature. The discussion, however, seems always to have been confined to the question of position and seems never to have been extended to the manner of fishing the flies. Individual characteristics or experiences led some to advocate a certain manner of manipulating the dropper-fly and others to recommend the sinking of the tail-fly to a greater depth; but the flies seems always to have been manipulated upon the theory that to be effective they must be constantly in motion. It seems to have been conceded by all that the flies should be always under the control and subject to the direction of the rod, thus enabling the angler to simulate living insects by twitching them over or under the surface of the water—a practice that is the exact opposite of the method of the dry fly fisher, who casts a single fly lightly upon the surface of the water and permits it to float with the current over or near the spot where he knows or believes a fish to lie.

Many expert wet fly anglers in this country have been using the floating fly for years, but most of them use it only on water where they consider it may prove more effective than the wet fly—usually upon the quiet surface of a pool or on flat, slow water. Contrary to the prevailing notion, however, the floating fly is not a whit more deadly on water of this character than the wet fly, when the latter is properly fished. The difficulty in taking trout on such water may be ascribed to two causes: (1) When the water is low and clear, or where it has little motion and the surface is unruffled, the fish is likely to perceive the activities of the angler at a greater distance than is possible in rougher water, and is thus sooner warned of his approach. (2) When the angler has been careful to conceal himself from the fish, the fly cast in the usual wet fly manner is likely to be refused because of its unnatural action, the wake made by dragging the flies across the smooth surface being sufficient at times to deter even small fish from becoming interested in it. The floating fly is far more effective than the wet, "jerky" fly, because, as no motion is imparted to it, it is more lifelike in appearance. When such a fly, properly presented, is refused such refusal may be due as much to a disinclination upon the part of the fish to feed as to his suspicion having been aroused. The wet fly fished *sunk,* with no more motion given to it than is given to the floating one (a single fly being used in each case), will prove quite as deadly as the latter on smooth water; and where many casts with the dry fly may be necessary to induce a rise, the sunk fly may appeal upon the first or second attempt, because its taking demands of the fish no particular exertion. The effort of the angler to impart a "lifelike" motion to the wet fly upon the surface will often be quite enough in itself to defeat his purpose. Such effort should never be made on clear, glassy water, for, while it may occasionally be successful, unseen fish are put down.

For many years I was one of those who firmly believed that only the smooth, slow stretches of a stream could be fished successfully with the dry fly. Experience, however, has taught me that the floater, skilfully handled, is applicable to any part of a swift stream short of a perpendicular waterfall. My unorthodox method of using it—which may be described as creating a whole family of flies instead of imitating an individual member thereof—may be characterised by some as "hammering" or "flogging," and condemned as tending to make fish shy because the leader is shown so often. My answer to this is that if the blows struck by the fly are light no harm is done. And, furthermore, if showing gut to the fish really tends to make them more wary, the sport of taking them, in my estimation, is pushed up a peg.

It is not my purpose to contend that the dry fly is more effective than the wet fly, although I do believe that, under certain conditions, the dry fly will take fish that may not be taken in any other manner. I do contend, however, that a greater fascination attends its use. All game birds are pursued with the same weapon, but the more difficult birds to kill have the greater attraction for sportsmen; and my predilection for the dry fly is based on the same principle.

My first dry fly was cast over the Junction Pool—the meeting of the waters of the Willowemoc and the Mongaup—about fifteen years ago, and the fact that I cast it at all was due more to the exigency of the occasion than to any predevised plan for attempting the feat. Every day in the late afternoon or evening I noted four or five fish rising in the pool formed by these two streams, and repeated attempts upon my part to take one of them by the old method absolutely failed me, although I put forth diligent efforts. The desire to take one of these fish became an obsession, and their constant rising to everything but my flies exasperated me to the point of wishing that I might bring myself to the use of dynamite.

One evening in looking through my fly book I found in one of the pockets a clipping from the *Fishing Gazette,* which I had placed there during the preceding winter. If my memory serves me, I think this article was entitled "Casting to Rising Fish." At any rate, the caption was such that it caught my eye, as it seemed to suggest the remedy for which I was searching. The article proved to be an account of the experience of an angler who used the dry fly for trout, and his exposition of the manner of using it seemed so clear that I determined to try it myself upon the pool over the rising fish in the late afternoon. Barring my inability to execute properly the things the author described and that I was called upon to do, the only stumbling-block in my way was the impossibility of my obtaining an artificial fly that resembled the insects upon which the trout were feeding, and the author laid a great deal of stress upon the necessity of using such an imitation.

I remember that, in a measure, I was mildly glad of this, because I felt that I would have an excuse for failure if I were unsuccessful. I "doctored" some wet flies into what I thought to be a fair imitation of the dry fly by tying the wings forward so that they stood at right angles to the body, and then sallied forth to the pool. On my way to the stream I went alternately hot and cold betwixt hope and fear. I rehearsed in my mind all the things I had to do, and I think I was coldest when I thought of having to float the fly. The writer had recommended the use of paraffin-oil as an aid to buoyancy, and this commodity was about as easily procurable in Sullivan County at that time as the philosopher's stone; in my then frame of mind the latter would probably have proven quite as good a buoyant. The pool was but a stone's throw from the house, and I arrived there in a few minutes, only to find a boy disturbing the water by dredging it with a worm. Him I lured away with a cake of chocolate, sat down to wait for the rise which came on shortly, and by the time I was ready there were a half dozen good fish feeding on the surface. I observed two or three sorts of flies about and on the water, to none of which my poor, mussed-up Queen-of-the-Waters bore the slightest resemblance. This did not deter me, however, and I waded boldly out to a position some forty feet below and to the right of the pool. My first cast amazed me. The fly alighted as gently as a natural insect upon the surface, and, watching it as it floated down toward the spot where a fish had been rising, I saw it disappear, a little bubble being left in its place. Instinctively I struck, and to my astonishment found that I was fast in a solid fish that leaped clear of the water. The leaping of this fish was a new experience, as I had never seen a trout jump as cleanly from the water. After a few flights and a determined rush or two I netted him—a rainbow trout just over a foot long and the first I had ever taken. This variety of trout had been placed in the stream a few years before as an experiment, and few had been caught. Stowing my prize in my creel, I prepared for another attempt as soon as the excitement in the pool had subsided. The fly I had used was bedraggled and slimy and would not float, so I knotted on another. My second attempt was as successful as the first, and I finally netted, after a tussle, a beautiful native trout that weighed a little over one pound. Four fine fish fell to my rod that evening, all within half an hour, and the fly was taken on the first cast each time. If such had not been the case I doubt very much if I should have succeeded, because I am certain that my confidence in the method would have been much weakened had I failed to take the first fish, and my subsequent attempts might not have been made at all, or, if made, would probably have ended in failure.

For several years after my first experience with the floating fly I used it in conjunction with the wet fly, and until I read Mr. Halford's "Dry Fly Fishing in Theory and Practice," when recognising his great authority and feeling that the last word had been said upon the subject, I used the dry fly only on such water as I felt he would approve of and fished only rising fish. Some time later on I read George A. B. Dewar's "Book of the Dry Fly." Mr. Dewar says: "I shall endeavour to prove in the course of this volume that the dry fly is never an affectation, save when resorted to in the case of brawling, impetuous streams of mountainous districts, where it is practically impossible of application." Here again I felt inclined to listen to the voice of authority and felt that I must abandon the dry fly. I was accustomed to fish such streams as Beaverkill, Neversink, Willowemoc, and Esopus, in New York; the Brodhead and Shohola, in Pennsylvania; the Saco and its tributaries, in New Hampshire, and others of similar character—all brawling, impetuous, tumbling streams—and it seemed to me that by continuing to use the dry fly on them I was profaning the creed of authority and inviting the wrath of his gods upon my head. Since then, however, I have continued the use of the dry fly on all of these streams, and a number of years ago abandoned the use of the wet fly for all time.

Since I began casting the fly over the streams of the region I have mentioned their character has greatly changed in many particulars, and conditions are not the same as they were twenty years ago. The natural streams themselves have changed; the condition of the water flowing in them has changed; the sorts of fish inhabiting the waters have changed; and the methods of taking the fish have changed, or should change; and it is to show why this last is true that the following pages are written.

The changes that have taken place in the character of our mountain streams may be attributed to many causes, chief of which, however, is the destruction of the timber which at one time covered the hills through which they have their course. During the frequent and long-continued droughts the denuded hills, baked hard as rock, shed the occasional summer showers as readily as the back of the proverbial duck; the streams become turbid torrents for a few hours, after which they run down, seemingly to a lower mark than before. So long as the forests covered the watersheds the rains as they fell were soaked up by the loose and porous earth about the roots of the trees, were cooled in the shade of the leaves and branches, and slowly percolated into the tiny brooklets through which they were fed to the streams for many days. Under present conditions the temperature of the streams is much higher than formerly, and, while the temperature has seldom risen to a point where it has been fatal to the fish, it has risen in many streams to a point that is distasteful to the native brook-trout (*Salvelinus fontinalis*).

It is not unreasonable to assume that the heat of the water has a very deleterious effect upon the vitality of the fish during certain years when the droughts are long sustained and, should the condition have existed for a great length of time prior to the spawning season, that the progeny for the year would probably come into being lacking the vitality necessary to overcome the attacks of natural enemies and disease. A bad spawning season, of course, reduces the hatch for the year, but is ordinarily not noticed by the angler until two or three years later, at which time the unusually small number of immature fish taken becomes a matter of comment among the frequenters of the streams. A native angler who has made it a practice to visit the spawning-grounds of trout for over twenty-five years stated to me that during the season of 1910 the redds were occupied by trout, but that not a fish spawned on any

of them in a stretch of nearly a mile of the stream which
flows past his home and which was under his constant
observation during the entire season. It is difficult for me
to believe that such a thing could have been possible, yet
I know the man to be a careful and accurate observer, and
his statement must be given credence. He seemed frightened at the prospect and alarmed as to the future of the
stream, and he besought me for an explanation of the
condition—which I was unable to give. My diary for that
year had been destroyed, so that I was then, and am now,
unable to even theorise as to whether or not the failure to
spawn was due to weather conditions prevailing at that
time. Let us hope, assuming that my informant was not
mistaken, that the curious condition observed by him was
confined to the stretch of the stream that he investigated.
Let us hope, further, that the fish, even in that stream, will
not become addicted to such an ungenerous and unnatural
habit.

Great numbers of trout must be destroyed in the periodi-
cal freshets that carry masses of ice tearing and grinding
over the beds of the mountain streams. When the ice breaks
up gradually there is very little danger to the fish; but a
sudden and continued thaw, accompanied by a steady
fall of warm rain, washes the snow from the hillsides,
swells the streams into wild torrents, and rips the very
bottom out of them. Any one who has witnessed the forming of an ice-jam and its final breaking must marvel at the
possibility of any fish or other living thing in its path
escaping destruction, so tremendous is the upheaval. A
few years ago a jam and freshet on the Brodhead, besides

uprooting [...] banks, lifted three iron bridges [...] s from their stone abutments and carried [...] a hundred yards down-stream, leaving them, [...] , mere masses of twisted iron. These bridges were twelve or fifteen feet above the normal flow of the stream, yet, even so, they did not escape destruction. How, then, is it possible for stream life to stand against such catastrophe? Furthermore, this scouring of the beds of the streams by ice and debris carried down during the floods undoubtedly destroys great quantities of the larvæ of the aquatic insects which form an important part of the trout's food, and this, too, indirectly affects the supply of fish available to the angler's rod. After a severe winter and a torrential spring there is a noticeable dearth of fly upon the water—another of the many causes of lament of the fly fisherman of to-day.

Directly or indirectly, all of the conditions above described are the result of the ruthless cutting of the timber from the hills. Happily, there is reason to hope that these conditions are not going to grow worse, because the present movement toward the preservation of the forests seems to be gaining headway; conservation of nature's resources will come to be a fixed policy of our National and State Governments, and if the policy is pushed with vigour and persistence our children's children may some day see our old familiar streams again singing gaily through great woods like those our fathers knew.

With the elements, man, beast, and bird all intent upon its destruction, it is a marvel that our native brook-trout survives. But live on he does, though his numbers constantly decrease. The great gaps left in his ranks are being filled by the alien brown trout—his equal in every respect but that of beauty. True, there is a wide difference of opinion in this particular, and there are some who will go so far as to say that the brown trout is, all round, the better fish for the angler. When feeding he takes the fly quite as freely as the native trout, leaps vigorously when hooked, grows rapidly to a large size, and seems better able to withstand abnormal changes in the temperature of the water, which are so often fatal to *fontinalis.* No one deplores the scarcity of our own beautiful fish more than I do; but we must not be blind to the facts that the brown trout is a game-fish, that he is in our streams and there to stay, and that our streams are suited to him. He is a fish of moods and often seems less willing to feed than the native trout; but for that reason alone, if for no other, I would consider him the sportier fish. When both varieties are taking freely and their fighting qualities compared, it is not easy to decide which is the gamer. The leaping of the brown trout is often more impressive than the determined resistance of the native trout, and the taking of a particularly active or particularly sluggish fish of either variety is frequently made the basis for an opinion. It seems to me that, in any event, the taking of even a single fair fish of either variety on the fly is an achievement to be put down as a distinct credit to the angler's skill and something to be proud of and to remember. Our native brook-trout is much loved of man. It has come to be something more than a fish: it is an ideal. It will always hold first place in the hearts of many anglers. I fear, however, that it must yield first place in the streams to its European contemporary, he having been endowed by nature with a constitution fitted to contend against existing conditions and survive.

My many years' experience upon the streams of New York and Pennsylvania have brought me to realise that changed conditions call for an expertness of skill and knowledge that anglers of the past generation did very well without. The streams now are smaller, the fish in them fewer and warier, and the difficulties of the angler who would take them greater. Three flies fished down-stream may still be a permissible method for those who pursue the trout of the wilderness, but the sportsman should now be willing to adopt the use of the single light surface fly when pursuing the trout of our domestic waters; and, if he does adopt it, as he gains in skill he will come at last to realise that it has a virtue not possessed by its wet brother. I can illustrate my point best by quoting an experience of my own that happened several years ago.

One day, while fishing an up-State stream, I met a dear old clergyman, who, after watching me for a long time, came up and said: "Young man, I have fished this stream for nearly forty years, and they will tell you at the house that I have been accounted as good as any man who ever fished here with a fly. I have killed some fine fish, too; but in all that time I have never been able to take trout as regularly as you have taken them in the few days you have been here. I am told that you use the dry fly and have some particular patterns. If it is not asking too much, will you be good enough to give me their names and tell me where they may be obtained?" I gave him the information he asked, and volunteered some instruction by pointing out that his gear was not suitable for the work, convincing him that such was the case by placing my own rod in his hands. We sat in the shade for a couple of hours exchanging ideas, and to prove or explode a theory of mine he agreed to fish a certain pool with me later in the day. He used my rod and rose and killed a brown trout of one pound five ounces, a little later leaving the fly in a heavier fish. He was an expert at placing the fly, but, not being used to the stiffer rod and lighter gut, he struck too hard, with the resultant smash. Being a good angler, he easily overcame this difficulty. He now fishes only with a rod of fine action and power, which enables him to place his fly easily, delicately, and accurately a greater distance that was possible with the "weeping" rod he formerly used. This he abandoned once and for all, and with it the wet fly. He came into the knowledge and enjoyment of the dry fly method, and he has since then frankly admitted to me that he greatly regretted having realised so late in life that the actual taking of trout constitutes but a very small part of the joy of fly fishing.

CHAPTER II
THE VALUE OF OBSERVATION

S EVERAL years ago I was looking on at a tennis match between the champion of America and one of the best men England ever sent to this country, and as I watched their play I could not help but marvel at the accuracy with which the players placed their shots. Their drives were wonderful for direction and speed. On nearly every return the ball barely cleared the net and was seldom more than a few inches above the top as it passed over. A friend who knew many of the experts told me how they attained to their remarkable precision. It was the custom of many of them, he said, when preparing for the big matches, to practise for accuracy by driving the ball against a wall. He said this was particularly true of the American champion, and that it was not unusual for him to use up a dozen or more balls in a day's practice. The wall had painted across its face a line of contrasting colour at a height from the ground equivalent to that of the top of a regulation tennis net, and upon the line were painted a number of disks about ten inches in diameter. Standing at a distance from the wall equivalent to the distance of the base-line of a regulation tennis-court from the net, the player would return the ball on its rebound from the wall,

15

striving each time to so place it that it would strike just above the line. The accomplishment of a satisfactory score after a succession of drives would convince the player that he had good control of his stroke, and he would then turn his attention to the disks, against each of which he would drive twenty or more shorts, taking them in turn and keeping a record of hits in each case. The accuracy developed by such practice was truly remarkable, and I hesitate to mention the number of times in succession one expert made clean hits—it seemed an incredible number.

I have seen golfers practising the weak places in their game for hours with as much zeal and earnestness as if they were playing a match, and a polo player of my acquaintance practises his strokes upon a field at his home, riding his ponies as daringly and recklessly as though a championship depended upon his efforts. The devotees of these and similar active sports are keenly alive to the necessity of constant practice, that spirit of competition which is so much a part of them making any endeavour that will aid toward high efficiency, or improve game or form, seem worth while. And in all sports, particularly those in which the competition is individual, whenever and wherever opportunity presents itself there will be found hundreds of enthusiasts following every play of the expert, keenly studying his method, observing his form, and absorbing and storing the knowledge so gained for their own practice later on court or field. So, too, even though competition has no place in fly fishing, and should have none, the angler ought to strive always to "play a good game." He should practise the tactics of his art with the same zeal as do the followers of competitive sports if he hopes ever to become an expert fly fisherman in the highest sense of that much misused term.

The casual angler who looks upon fishing as merely incidental to his periods of recreation, during which his chief concern is the recuperation of tired brain and unstrung nerves, may feel that he is making a business of his pleasure by devoting much time to the study of his angling. In a measure, this is true, and it would be asking much, indeed, of him who thinks of fly fishing only as a pastime. But to him who realises that it is a sport—a sport that is also an art— there is no incident, complex or simple, that is unworthy of his attention and consideration. No sport affords a greater field for observation and study than fly fishing, and it is the close attention paid to the minor happenings upon the stream that marks the finished angler. The careless angler frequently overlooks incidents, or looks upon them as merely trivial, from which he might learn much if he would but realise their meaning at the time.

Of greatest importance to the dry fly angler is that mastery of the rod and line that enables him to place his fly lightly and accurately upon the water. I venture to assert that one who has had the advantage of expert instruction in handling a rod, and is thereby qualified to deliver a fly properly, will raise more trout upon his first attempt at fishing a stream than another who, though he knows thoroughly the haunts and habits of the fish, casts indifferently. The contrast between the instructed novice and the uninstructed veteran would be particularly noticeable were they to cast together over the same water in which fish were rising freely. Whether or not the novice would take more fish than the veteran is another question. Lacking experience, the novice would probably hook few fish and land fewer. But he would be starting right, and the necessity of overcoming later on that bad form likely to be acquired by all who begin without competent instruction would be eliminated, and the stream knowledge of the veteran would come to him in time.

The beginner should watch the expert at work and should study particularly the action of the rod. He should note that the power which impels the line forward starts from the butt, travels the entire length of the rod, is applied by a slight forward push rather than by a long sweep, and ends in a distinct snap. He will soon learn that the wrist must do the real work, and no better scheme for teaching this has ever been devised than the time-honoured one of holding a fly book or a stone between the casting arm and the body. The proper action of the rod will be best learned if he fasten that part of the butt below the reel to the forearm with a piece of string, a strap of leather, or a stout rubber band, the effect of which device will be to stop the rod in an almost perpendicular position when the line is retrieved. The pull of the line as it straightens out behind him will be distinctly felt, will give him a good idea of the power and action of his rod, and serve as a signal for the forward cast. He should practise casting as often as his spare time will allow—over water when possible, but over grass if necessary. He should not wait until the stream is reached and actual fishing problems begin to press upon his notice for solution. His mind will then be occupied with many other things; hence, the knack of handling the rod should have been already acquired.

After the beginner is satisfied that he can properly place and deliver his fly he should turn his attention to the study of the fish and the currents of the stream. If he has been a wet fly angler his experiences will stand him in good stead, as it will qualify him to locate the likely haunts of the fish. Long and varied though his experience may have been, however, the use of the dry fly will open avenues of observation and knowledge that were hidden from him while he practised the old method. My own experience is responsible for this rather broad statement, but not until after I had become an ardent advocate of the dry fly, and had abandoned the wet fly for good and all, did I realise the truth of it. In the beginning I was ever on the alert for rising fish, and, instead of boldly assailing promising water, wasted much time, on many occasions, scrutinising the water for some indication that a fish was feeding. In this way I frequently discovered non-feeding fish lying in places where I had not expected to find them. Such fish were then the more easily approached because I was able to assume a position myself that would not disclose my presence. Just as frequently, too, I have seen fine fish cruising about, and have taken many that might have been driven away by the slightest movement on my part. In many cases I have been compelled to remain absolutely motionless for ten or fifteen minutes before a fish would come to rest long enough to make worth while an attempt to get a fly to it. Nearly every time, too, that a fish has been hooked I have seen it actually take the fly—an action always instructive, because fish vary greatly in their manner of taking, and interesting, because in it lies one of the real charms of fly fishing.

The continued use of a floating fly upon water where the angler sees no indication of feeding fish, but where experience tells him that they may lie, seems to develop in him a remarkable keenness of vision. This is a direct result, perhaps, of the attention which he gives to his fly. My own experience is that while I am watching my fly float down-stream some stone of irregular formation, peculiar colour, or difference in size from others about it, lying upon the bottom, arrests my eye, with the effect of making the water appear shallower or clearer than it really is. My fly appears to be the centre of a small area ,upon the surface of the water through which everything is seen as clearly as through a water-glass, the shadow of the fly itself upon the bottom often being plainly discernible. Anglers who fish the dry fly learn to identify the living shadow that appears suddenly under the fly as a trout ready to take it on its next drift down-stream, and to recognise a fish as it sidles out from the bank or swings uncertainly toward the fly just as it passes the boulder that shelters him. In either case an interesting opportunity is afforded, particularly for exercising a very necessary attribute—self-control.

It may be that many happenings I now see upon the stream passed unnoticed when I used the wet fly because of some lack of concentration and observation. If this be so, I have the newer method to thank for the development of those faculties. I have learned not to overlook a single minor happening. Perhaps my keenness to ascribe some meaning to the slightest incident has resulted in the building of many very fine structures of theory and dogma upon poor foundations. This may be true, but I am certain that their weaknesses have always become apparent to me in time; and, on the other hand, I am just as certain that I have been greatly benefited by my habit of close attention to the little things that happen on the stream. For instance, I cherished the belief for many years that one advantage of up-stream fishing lay in the fact that when the fly was taken the hook was driven into the fish's mouth instead of being pulled away, as in down-stream fishing. I thought this to be one of the strongest arguments in favour of up-stream fishing, and, theoretically, it is. But I know now that many fish that take a floating fly do so when they are headed down-stream. While there are still many reasons why up-stream fishing is the better method, this particular argument no longer has weight with me.

As I remember it, the strongest admonition of my early schooling on the stream was never to remain long in one place. I was taught to believe that if a rise was not effected on the first few casts subsequent effort on that water was wasted—that the trout would take the fly at once or not at all. I clung to this belief for years, until one day I saw a fine fish lying in shallow water and took him after casting a dozen or more times. Since then I have taken fish after upward of fifty casts, and I rarely abandon an attempt for one that I can see if I feel certain that it has not discovered me. Even when I have not actually seen a fish, but have known or believed one to be lying near by, the practice has proven effective. Thus I have had the satisfaction of accomplishing a thing once believed to be impossible; but I have gained more than that: I have learned to be persevering and, what is still more important, deliberate. The man who hurries through a trout stream defeats himself. Not only does he take few fish but he has no time for observation, and his experience is likely to be of little value to him.

The beginner must learn to look with eyes that see. Occurrences of apparently little importance at the moment may, after consideration, assume proportions of great value. The taking of an insect, for instance, may mean nothing more than a rising trout; but the position occupied by this fish may indicate the position taken by others in similar water. The flash of a trout, changing his position preparatory to investigating the angler's fly, will frequently disclose the spot occupied by him before he changed his position; and, later on, when the fish are not in the keenest mood for feeding, a fly presented there accurately may bring a rise. The quick dart up-stream of a small trout from the tail of a pool is a pretty fair indication that a large fish occupies the deeper water above; it indicates just as certainly, however, that the angler has little chance of taking him, the excitement of the smaller fish having probably been communicated to his big relative.

The backwater formed by a swift current on the upstream side of a boulder is a favourite lurking-place of brown trout. I was fishing such places one day, and found the trout occupying them in rather a taking mood. In approaching a boulder which looked particularly inviting, and while preparing to deliver my fly, I was amazed to see the tail and half the body of a fine trout out of the water at the side of the rock. For a moment I could not believe that I had seen a fish—the movement was so deliberate—and I came to the conclusion that it was fancy or that a water-snake, gliding across the stream, had shown itself. Almost immediately, however, I saw the flash of a trout as he left the backwater and dashed pell-mell into the swift water at the side of the boulder. Down-stream he came until he was eight or ten feet below the rock, when, turning sharply and rising to the surface, he took from it some insect that I could not see. Up-stream again he went, and shortly resumed his position in the dead water, showing half his body as he stemmed the current at the side of the rock. Once more this performance was repeated, and I knew I had stumbled upon an interesting experience. Hastily measuring the distance, hoping to get my fly to him before some natural insect might excite him to give another exhibition of gymnastic feeding, I dropped it about three feet above him, and, contrary to my usual method of retrieving it as it floated past the up-stream side of the boulder, I permitted it to come down riding the top of the wave, when the same flash came as the trout dashed after it. The fish could be plainly seen almost directly under the fly. As it reached the rapidly flattening water below the rock, he turned and took it viciously, immediately darting up-stream again. He was soundly hooked, however, and I netted a fine fish lacking one ounce of being a pound and a half. My experience heretofore had been that if a fly were placed a yard or so above this point and allowed to float down to the rock a feeding fish would rush forward—often as much as two feet—and take it, immediately turning or backing into his position again. I had assumed from this observation that when the fly passed the rock or backwater without a rise it should be retrieved and another try made. This fish satisfied me, however, that when really feeding, or when inclined to feed, trout may be lured comparatively long distances by inviting-looking morsels. Either he did not decide to take the fly until just as it was passing him or else he liked the exercise of the chase. In any event, he was not peculiar in his habit, because four more fish were taken in the same manner the same day.

In most cases when the fly is cast above a boulder lying in swift water (which I consider, under certain conditions, one of the best places to look for brown trout) it will be taken as it approaches the rock, the trout darting out and retiring immediately to avoid being caught in the swifter water on either side of his stronghold. But if it is not taken, and is permitted to float down with the current, it may bring a response.

It was a somewhat similar observation which prompted the practice and, I must say, rather dubious development of what some of my friends are pleased to call the "fluttering" or "bounce" cast. This cast is supposed to represent the action of the fluttering insect, the fly merely alighting upon the water, rising, alighting again, repeating the movement three or four times at most; finally coming to rest and being allowed to float down-stream. It rarely comes off, but when it does it is deadly; and, for the good of the sport, I am glad that it is difficult, though sorry, too, for the pleasure of accomplishing it successfully is really greater than that of taking fish with it. The cast is made with a very short line—never over twenty-five feet—and the fly alone touches the water. The action of the fly is very similar to that produced by the method known as "dapping," but instead of being merely dangled from the rod, as is the case when "dapping," the fly is actually cast. It should be permitted to float as far as it will after its fluttering or skipping has ceased. The beginner practising the cast will do well to cast at right angles to the current, and he should choose rather fast water for his experimenting. The speed of the water will cause the fly to jump, and the action it should have will be the more readily simulated than if the first attempts are made on slow water.

I had made a flying trip to the Brodhead, and, with that strange fatality which seems so often to attend the unfortunate angler rushing off for a week-end in the early season, found the stream abnormally high and horrible weather prevailing. After many attempts to get into the stream, with results equally disastrous to my clothing and temper, I abandoned all idea of wading and walked and crawled along the bank, casting my fly wherever I could but rarely finding good water that could be reached, and rising but a few small fish. As there was a gale blowing in my face directly down-stream, it was practically impossible to place a fly where I wished with any delicacy, and I decided to abandon the sport after trying a pool just above me that I knew contained big fish. My first cast on this water, made during a lull, fell lightly, but brought no response, and after a further half dozen fruitless attempts I began to think of the fine log fire at the house. I made one more cast, however, this time in the teeth of the wind. Using but twenty-five feet of line and a short leader, I was able to straighten both in the air. The wind kept all suspended for an instant, the fly, accompanied by a small part of the leader, finally falling upon the water, where it remained but a fraction of a second, the wind whisking it off and laying it down a foot away. This happened five or six times as the fly came down-stream, and during the time it was travelling a distance of not over eight or ten feet five trout, each apparently over a pound in weight, rose to it, but missed because it was plucked away by the wind just in time to save them. I did not get one of them, and, as it was practically impossible to continue casting under the prevailing conditions, I left the stream. It was brought home solidly to me that day, however, that it was the *action* of the fly alone that moved the fish—and my day was not badly spent. I cannot say as much of the many other days since then that I have spent in what I feel were rather foolish attempts to imitate the effect produced by the wind on that day.

The study of the positions taken by big fish when they are feeding, and those which they occupy when they are not, is an important part of the education of the fly fisher. Each time the angler takes a good fish or sees one feeding, if he will note in his diary its position, the condition of the water, temperature, atmosphere, time of day, and the insect being taken, he will soon have an accumulation of data from which he may learn how to plan a campaign against particular fish at other times. Extremely interesting in itself, the study of insects is of great value to the angler in his attempts at imitation, and the information gleaned from autopsy might not be acquired in any other manner.

It may be said to be an axiom of the fly fisher that where a small trout is seen feeding rarely need a large one be looked for. But the actions of a small fish in sight may sometimes indicate the presence of a large one unseen. The taking of a fine trout on a certain stream in Sullivan County, on August 27, 1906, after one of those long periods of drought so common in recent years, convinced me of this. I had been waiting for even a slight fall of rain, and, quite a heavy shower having come up the evening before, I started for this stream. Upon my arrival there I was surprised to learn that not a drop of rain had fallen in weeks, and that the shower which had been heavy twenty miles away had not reached the vicinity. While driving from the station to the house at which I was to stop, along a road that paralleled the stream, the many glimpses I had of the latter filled me with misgivings. At one point the stream and road are very near each other, and, stopping my driver, I got out to look at a famous pool below a dam which had long outlived its usefulness. It was a sizzling-hot day, and at that time—eleven o'clock—the sun was almost directly overhead; yet in the crystal-clear water of this pool, with not a particle of shade to cover him, lay a native trout fourteen inches in length which afterward proved to weigh one pound three ounces. Too fine a fish, I thought, as I clambered back into the carriage, to be occupying such a place in broad daylight, and I promised myself to try for him later in the afternoon. Returning about six o'clock, I found him in the same position, and during the full twenty minutes I watched him, while he appeared to be nervously alert, he never moved. Notwithstanding the fact that everything was against me, and knowing that the chances were more than even that the fish would see me, my rod, or my line, I made my plans for approaching him; yet, busy as I was, I could not rid my mind of this ever-recurring thought: with all the known aversion of his kind to heat, and their love of dark nooks, why was this fish out in this place on such a day? Why did he not find a place under the cool shade of the dam? With the instinct strong within him to protect himself by hiding, the impulse must have been much stronger that forced him to take so conspicuous a stand—a mark to the animals which prey upon his kind. As there were absolutely no insects upon the water, and scarcely enough current to bring food of other sort to him, he could not have been feeding. The only reason, then, to account for his being there—the thought struck me forcibly enough—was his fear of a bigger fish. The logical conclusion was that if a fish of his inches (no mean adversary) exposed himself so recklessly the one that bullied him must be quite solid. I tested this fellow's appetite with a small, pinkish-bodied fly of my own invention, and, standing about forty feet below and considerably to the left, dropped it three or four feet above him; but, although it was certain he could see the fly, he made no attempt to go forward and take it. As it neared him, however, he rushed excitedly to the right and then to the left, taking the fly as it came directly over him, and, before I could realise what had happened, came down-stream toward me at a great rate. As he was securely hooked, I kept him coming, and netted him quietly at the lip of the pool.

That this fish did not take the fly the instant it fell meant to me that he was afraid to go forward into the deeper water which harboured his larger fellow; and his action as the fly appeared over him meant that, while he wanted it badly enough, he would not risk an altercation with the other, which might also have seen it. When he did finally decide that the coast was clear, he took it quickly and rushed down toward the shallower water where he might be secure against sudden attack.

If some of the theories developed in those few moments appear fanciful, it must be remembered that my mind was occupied with the thought that the pool contained a larger fish, and the conclusions based upon the subsequent actions of this smaller one only tended to strengthen this belief. Fanciful or not, I was rewarded a few minutes later by the sight of a monster tail breaking the surface just under the water that trickled over the apron of the dam. Having prepared a gossamer leader, preferring to risk a smash to not getting a rise, I dropped a small Silver Sedge —which I used because it could be more plainly kept in sight—almost immediately in the swirl and was at once fast in a lusty fish. After many abortive attempts to lead him into the diminutive net I had with me, I flung the thing, in disgust, into the woods. I finally beached the fish and lifted him out in my hand. He was a fine brown trout, eighteen and three quarter inches in length, and weighed, the next morning, two pounds nine ounces.

While I was engaged with this fish another rose in practically the same spot under the apron of the dam. Hurriedly replacing the bedraggled fly with a new one, I waited for the trout to show himself, which he did presently, and again I was fast—this time in one of the best fish I have ever seen in these waters. It seemed an interminable length of time, though probably not over ten minutes, that I was engaged with this one, and it was impossible to move him; he kept alternately boring to toward the dam and sulking. In one of the latter fits I urged him toward me somewhat too strongly, and he was off. Immediately I was afforded a sight of what I had lost as he leaped clear of the water in an evident endeavour to dislodge the thing that had fastened to his jaw. The smash made as he struck the water still resounds in my ear, and when I say that this fish would have gone close to five pounds I but exercise the right to that license accorded all anglers who attempt to describe the size of the big ones that get away. Having one good fish in my creel, however, I really had some basis for my calculation—at any rate, he was one of the best fish I have ever risen. Examining my leader, I found it had not broken, but the telltale curl at the end proved that, in the fast-gathering gloom, I had been careless in knotting on the fly.

CHAPTER III
THE RISE

A NY disturbance of the surface made by a trout is usually referred to as a "rise," but the characterisation is erroneous except where it is applied to fish feeding upon the surface. Rising fish are the delight of the dry fly fisher, but are really the easiest fish to take—provided, always, that no error is made in the presentation of the fly. The angler is called upon to exhibit a fine skill in casting, a knowledge of the insect upon which the fish is feeding, and to make the proper selection of an imitation; but he is aided materially by being apprised of the location of the fish, and is further helped by the knowledge that he is throwing to a willing one.

The study of the habits of rising fish, or, to use a more inclusive term, feeding fish—because a feeding fish may not be a rising one—is of the utmost importance to the dry fly enthusiast, who knows how difficult it is to induce a fish feeding on or near the bottom to rise to his floater.

Inasmuch as the principal literature available on this delightful branch of angling is the work of Englishmen who have, with unfailing unanimity, used the same terms in describing the positions and actions of feeding fish, it would be unwise to attempt to employ others, and for that reason I have made use of them throughout this chapter.

Compared with our swift-flowing water, the gentle, slow-moving, chalk streams of Southern England offer greater advantages to students of the habits of feeding fish, not only because of the greater deliberation with which the trout secures his food in them but also because a greater number of aquatic insects contribute to his sustenance there than are found on our swift streams; consequently, the English student has far greater opportunity for observation. The water-weeds grow so heavily on these English streams that at times it is found necessary to cut them out to some extent if fly fishing is to be pursued. These weeds harbour great numbers of snails, shrimps, larvæ, etc., of which the trout are inordinately fond, and when the fish are seeking this luscious fare the trials of the angler fishing with a floating fly are, indeed, many. Trout feeding in this manner are described as "tailing" fish, from the fact that the tail of the fish is observed breaking the surface of the water violently or gently, as the case may demand, in his efforts to secure or dislodge his prey. Heavy weed growth being unusual on our swift streams, the trout do not have the same opportunity to feed in the manner described as their English cousins, and, consequently, the American fly fisherman is not particularly interested in tailing fish; but it must not be forgotten that caddis larvæ abound in our waters, and that trout occasionally pick up crawfish, snails, and other *Crustacea* and *Mollusca* from the bottom, usually in the less rapid parts of the stream. Fish so feeding do break the surface with their tails, and, even though the tail be not actually seen, the action of this fin in maintaining the fish's equilibrium causes a swirl which is often mistaken for a rise. A trout often shows his tail in rapid water but this is occasioned by the necessity of forcing his head down to overcome the force of the current after he has taken food of some sort upon the surface or just below it, and the action must not be confused with that of a fish feeding upon the bottom in the more quiet stretches.

The term "bulging" is applied to fish that are feeding below the surface upon the nymphæ of insects about to undergo the metamorphosis which produces the winged fly. The trout is a very busy fellow at this time, and covers left, centre, and right field with equal facility; but he occasionally misses, and at the instant of his viciously breaking the surface of the water the insect may be seen taking its laboured flight—escaping by a hair's breadth the death which pursued it. When trout are feeding in this manner the angler's patience is taxed to the utmost, and after a succession of flies has been tried without success the discomfited angler may be excused if he concludes that his artificial is not a good imitation. He may not be far wrong.

Although aside from the main subject of dry fly fishing, I will in this connection attempt to show how the sunk fly may be used successfully against the "bulger." As the nymph is still enclosed in its shuck, or case, it is quite obvious that an artificial fly made with wings is not an imitation of it. Consequently, a hackle-fly should be used even though it, too, is a poor imitation. A suggestion of the general hue of the natural is quite sufficient. The cast is made some distance above the feeding fish, so that the fly will approach the trout approximately as the nymph would, *i. e.*, under water and rising. If no attempt be made to impart motion the fly drifting with the current will be more natural in its action than the angler can hope to make it appear by manipulation. Besides, the trout is an excellent judge of pace, and, making for a natural-looking morsel, is sorely disappointed and not likely to come again if it is jerked away from him at the moment he is about to take it. One fly only should be used, and quite as much care is required in its delivery as would be necessary were a floating fly being presented. Errors made in casting are more readily concealed by the current in the case of the sunk fly.

When the attention of the fish is fixed upon insects beneath the surface it is difficult to attract his notice to a floating fly, except, perhaps, at such times as the fly appears before him when he is close to the surface; but it can be done—and in two ways. Fish so feeding are moving about, darting here and there taking nymphæ. A swirl made by the fish in all likelihood only marks the place where he was, and he may be a yard or more up-stream, or to right or left, where he went to secure the nymph. If the swirl is made by his tail at the time he starts for the insect and not at the moment he takes it, there is little knowledge as to his actual position to be gained from the disturbance; the only indication is that he is feeding. The angler must be able to distinguish between the disturbance made by a bulger feeding under water and that made by a fish taking a winged insect upon the surface—often not a very difficult thing to do—and he must conduct his campaign accordingly. The signs of the surface-feeding fish are easily discernible to the quick eye. The gentle rise in slow water, or the swifter rush where the fly is in the current, starts a ripple immediately from the centre made by the nose or mouth of the fish, and, of course, is unmistakable where the actual taking of the insect is seen. In all cases the surface is broken. The commotion made by the bulging fish is started under water, and, while the disturbance is ultimately seen upon the surface, the form it assumes is more of a swirl or boil and is quite unlike the concentric rings that mark the actual breaking of the surface.

Occasionally, as I have said, the "fielder muffs the fly," and this is the moment that, if the angler be alert, an artificial fly dropped immediately over the fish is likely to meet with a hearty welcome. I am convinced that a trout that misses his prey in this manner frequently stays on the spot where he lost it long enough to give the angler an opportunity to present his fly, if he is within striking distance—and ready. He must be prompt in making his throw, however, because the fish may have his attention attracted elsewhere at any moment. If a rise be not effected at once the angler should not try again immediately, because the possibility of the fish having left his position, or of having been scared by the line, or of frightening another which may have come between, is too great to make the attempt worth while.

When fish are feeding all over the pool, and the angler is impatient and not content to stand idly by waiting for an opportunity such as described, let him try the following method: He should look the water over carefully, keep out of it if possible, and choose the spot where the fly is to be placed. Knowledge of the water and of the habits of the fish will guide him in this choice, but he should not cast to the swirl. Having chosen his water, which should be toward the head of the pool, not much above its centre, and preferably where the current will carry the fly down faster than the leader (the choice being governed naturally by the character of the stretch), he should place his fly some distance—a yard or two—ahead of the swirl and a foot or two to the side nearest him, allowing it to float down eight or ten feet; if no rise is effected he should place his fly in the same spot again and again until he has made twenty-five casts or more. It is important that each cast should be executed with the same precision and delicacy as marked the first attempt.

The method is based upon the theory that a feeding trout—or even one that is not feeding, for that matter—may be induced to take up a position in line with the direction in which the angler's fly is travelling, under the belief that flies are coming down-stream in such quantities as to make them worth investigating. Once this position is compelled it is only a question of time and patience upon the part of the angler. The trout will rise eventually to one of this "hatch." The angler cannot hope to have this *coup* come off, however, if he has made any mistake in his casting or has shown himself or his rod.

The beginner practising the method will find it most difficult to restrain an almost uncontrollable impulse to leave off casting in the one spot in order to place his fly over the swirl made by some other fish. If he gives way to that impulse he courts failure—and down comes the house he is building. It is quite likely that a trout is preparing to investigate the "hatch" at the very moment the angler changes his water, and, of course, will be frightened away by seeing the rod or the line which is thrown over it to the other fish. The method usually employed by the novice is productive of nothing. Because many feeding fish are seen, he hurriedly casts over this one, then over that one, in the hope that his fly will be taken, and finally gives up in despair when his hope is not realised.

If a mistake unfortunately occurs—the danger of which naturally increases in proportion to the number of casts made—it is quite useless to carry the attempt further. The angler should retire for a few moments or continue a bit farther up or down stream, selecting a spot some distance from where he began, and always bearing mind the necessity for throwing above and to the near side of the swirl. If no mistake is made the chances are at least even that those early evening "rises" which have so long mocked his skill may show a profit. The angler, however, may spend a profitable quarter hour watching the insects upon the water or rising from it, and catching some for closer examination. During this time, if there is a cessation of swirls, as there likely will be, it indicates that the nymphæ are becoming fewer and that, the "hatch" being over for the present, his last chance has come for a try at the bulgers. He should proceed, as before, to create his artificial "hatch," and he will have even a better chance of success because the attention of the trout will be less occupied.

In selecting water in which to place the fly, in order to take bulging fish by the method I have suggested, the angler will do well to choose that where the current is swift but the surface unbroken; and too much stress cannot be laid upon the importance of having the fly float down as nearly as possible in the same lane and position each time. When the trout has ceased feeding upon the nymphæ his opportunity for casting to fish that are really rising is come, and he may try these until darkness drives him home.

One who has observed trout feeding upon the tiny *Diptera* called indiscriminately by anglers "black gnats," "punkies," "midges," etc., is quite inclined to believe that, while "smutting" is rather an inelegant term to apply to the fish, the insects themselves, considering the provocation, have been let off too lightly in being described as "smuts" and "curses." These diminutive pests seem to be abroad at all times of the day, but are particularly numerous in the late afternoon, when clouds of them may be seen hovering over the still water of the pools. At such times the trout seem to be busily feeding, but the keenest observation does not disclose what it is they are taking. These "curses" are so small that it seems incredible that large trout should be interested in them. That they are is easily proven by autopsy, and I have found solid masses of them in the gullets and stomachs of sizable fish, proving that they must have been extremely busy if the insects were taken singly. If one could see these tiny things upon the water, and could see a trout rise to them, he would have convincing evidence that they are taken singly; but, though my eyesight is still good, I have never been able to satisfy myself that I have actually seen a fish take one of them. After many experiences with trout under such conditions, and particularly after a series of observations extending on one occasion over a period of four successive days, I am almost ready to believe that the fish do not wait for them to fall upon the water. This notion—perhaps fanciful— came to me while on a pool that had been my objective during an afternoon's fishing, and upon which I intended to close the day. Arriving there about a half hour before sundown, I was not a little delighted to find fish rising freely all over. After studying them for a few moments I concluded that they were not "bulging," because the surface was broken each time with a distinct "smack." They could not have been "tailing" because the water was about four feet deep. They were not rising to any insects that I could see, although I looked long and steadily. Yet they rose freely, and each fish rose again and again in practically the same spot.

Using the smallest fly that I had with me, a flat-winged "black gnat" tied on a No. 16 hook, I cast faithfully but unavailingly for some time, endeavoring to interest two fish which were nearest me, and until I was quite ready to confess myself beaten. However, I decided to try them with a larger fly, and while preparing to tie this on my attention was attracted by four distinct clouds of insects hovering over the water—on the wing, certainly, but making no flight. They were merely dancing in the air about two feet above the pool. Watching closely, I saw the insects gradually decrease this distance until but an inch or two separated the lower extremity of a cloud of them from the water, when directly underneath would come another "smack" as the tail of a trout broke the surface. Immediately the swarm would scatter, though but for an instant, collecting again to perform the same evolution as before, when again they would be scattered by a fish under them. This happened to all four swarms in rapid succession, and it was quite evident that a trout was under each. Every time the insects were close to the water the tail of a trout would be seen and water would be thrown amongst them. Query: Did the trout deliberately throw water at these insects with the intention of drenching those within reach and in order that they might be picked up at leisure after they had fallen into the stream? And, if so, why were the fish not observed in the act of picking them up? Or did the sight of the insects excite the anger of the fish, or a sport-loving instinct—if, indeed, fish are capable of these emotions?

My subsequent experience with these fish tended only to confuse me further in my guessing. This "spattering" game went on for fifteen or twenty minutes, and was brought to a conclusion, finally, by the retirement of the "curses," which left the scene perpendicularly, going straight up until lost to view. After they had disappeared the fish stopped rising. Having marked them down, I determined to have one more try with a large fly, and, to my amazement, my first cast brought a swift rise, but no connection was made. Resting the fish for a moment, I tried him again; he rose, and I was fast in what appeared to be a very good fish. I had great difficulty in leading him to the lower end of the pool, so that I might not disturb the others, and finally netted him. He proved to be a small trout and was hooked on the side just above the tail. I then tried the others, and, although I rose each one at least three times, I hooked none, nor on any occasion did I feel that the fly had been touched. By this time it was quite dark and I left for home.

On the three following days I met with the same experience. I had innumerable rises to my fly after the "curses" had left, hooked but one fish each evening, and, by a remarkable coincidence, each foul and near the tail. Again, query: Was this mere accident or were the trout trying to drench my fly? Were they still on the lookout for the sport afforded them by the clouds of insects? The gullets of the fish taken were lined with the small insects, the stomachs also being well filled with them; but how the fish took them after they had risen without my seeing some indication of it, I cannot imagine. I feel quite certain that they were not taken at the instant of the rise, because the insects did not touch the water at any time; nor did the trout show any part of their bodies above the surface except their tails. So they could not have been taken in the air. Some day, perhaps, the problem may be solved, but at present I have no solution to offer.

A bulging or smutting fish and a cursing angler are not a rare combination. If there is anything more perplexing and vexing than the sight of fish rising all about and one's best efforts going unrewarded, I cannot imagine what it is.

A bulging fish may be taken with an imitation of the

insects he is feeding upon, either sunk in one form or floating in another; but a smutting fish cannot be appealed to with any imitation of his food of the moment. The colour of the pests may be imitated, but no ingenuity of man can fashion an artificial so that it will resemble in size the minute form of the natural; and, even if ingenuity could do it, the hook to be used in conformity would be absolutely useless and probably quite as difficult to make as the fly. Lacking a correct imitation of the "curses," which, even if good, might not be taken, one may accept the rebuffs offered to his fly with an equanimity born of the knowledge that he is not alone in his trouble.

If smutting fish are to be taken at all they will probably be taken on a fly that has no resemblance to any particular insect except, perhaps, one that is indigenous to the stream, or one in which the angler has faith. It may assume any form, flat-winged or erect. Colour, of course, is not important, except that it should not be too brilliant, a fly of sombre hue, such as the Whirling Dun, Cahill, or Evening Dun, being very effective, the Gold-Ribbed Hare's Ear or Wickham's Fancy frequently being accepted. I am inclined to think that a small fly receives no more attention than a large one, if as much; but nothing larger than a No. 12 or No. 14 hook should be used.

Meeting with failure while the insects are about, the angler should rest until they have disappeared and then, having marked the position of the fish, try them with the method described for bulgers. Failing again, let him figure it out if he can.

When fish are feeding upon some particular species of

insect it is quite logical to assume that an imitation of that species will appeal to them more readily than an imitation of any other. But when the insects are numerous, as they are on occasions, and the fish are moving about, the chance of the artificial fly being selected from among the great number of naturals upon the water is one to whatever the number may be. As a general rule, the larger fish take up positions which by virtue of might are theirs for the choosing and almost invariably in places where many flies are carried down by the current. If they be rising steadily the angler is enabled to reduce the odds against him by his ability to place his fly near the spot where he knows one to be lying. It does not follow, however, that because certain insects are observed flying about they are the species with which the trout are engaged for the moment.

If an insect be observed flying as though it had some objective point in view, it may be safely concluded that it has but recently assumed the winged state. In this case it is attractive to the fish only at the moment it emerges from its shuck, or immediately afterward while it is resting upon the water, for the very obvious reason that it does not appear upon the water again until it is about to deposit its eggs, if a female, or, if of the opposite sex, when it falls lifeless after the fulfilment of its natural duties.

When the insects are seen dancing about over the water, oftentimes a considerable height above it—in some cases thirty feet or more—the observer may be quite satisfied that they are the perfect males of the species waiting for the females to appear. After the sexual function has been completed the female may be seen flitting over the water,

dipping to the surface and rising again, in the act of de-
positing her eggs, finally coming to rest as the function is
completed, only to be swept away to her death. As she
does not travel any considerable distance during this last
act of her life, she proves of greatest interest to the fish at
this stage of it.

One who observes closely will see that at the moment
the female approaches the water, or during her subsequent
dips, attempts, frequently successful, are made by the fish
to capture her. As these efforts require some activity, they
are resorted to usually by the more agile dandiprats. The
larger fish are quite as interested in the dainty morsel as
are their younger brothers, but they do not make the same
frantic efforts to secure it, preferring to attend the fly
closely in its movements until the opportunity presents
itself to take it with little or no exertion. This is usually at
the time ovipositing is about completed or the fly is resting
upon the surface of the water preparatory to another flight.
The females of some species are less active in the performance of this duty than those of others. They select the
more placid stretches of the stream, ride quietly upon its
surface, and the eggs exude from the oviduct as they sail
along. Occasionally, after traveling in this manner for a
time, they rise from the water, fly a short distance, and
settle again. They are incapable of guiding themselves and
are naturally carried along by the current and over the fish.

It has been my observation that during the period of
ovipositing a great majority of the insects are headed
directly up-stream, instinctively knowing, perhaps, that
contact with the current in that position will more readily

relieve them of their burdens. And, while I have no certain knowledge that it is so, I am inclined to believe that the setæ or hair-like tail enables them to assume and maintain this position. At any rate, it should be the angler's ambition to imitate this action, and present his counterfeit with its tail or hook end coming down to the fish. This gives the added advantage of having the business end taken first and eliminates the danger of disturbing the fish by having the shadow of the leader thrown over him in advance. To do it successfully calls for a nicety of judgment in the handling of rod and line; but when the skill is acquired its successful execution has its own reward.

The utmost caution should be used in approaching a feeding fish. The danger of putting him down does not depend solely upon his getting sight of the angler; he may also be apprised of the angler's coming by the excited darting up-stream of smaller fish which have been below him. If the character of the water to be fished indicates that other and smaller fish may be hidden, or if their presence be disclosed by *their* feeding, it is much safer to cast at right angles to the selected fish than to attempt to cast from below and over the smaller ones. If the situation demands that the fly be placed from this position it should be floated down to the fish from a point two or three feet above and should not be cast directly over him. Inasmuch as the trout is more likely to see the rod at this angle, a longer line should be thrown than would otherwise be necessary and, if the fish has been well spotted, great care must be exercised in presenting the fly without undue accompaniment of leader.

The fly may be presented alone by using the horizontal cast. If an attempt is being made to drop the fly three feet above the fish, it is necessary to aim at a spot six feet above, with a bit longer line than will just reach, suddenly checking the cast at the very end as it straightens. This will have the effect of throwing the fly down-stream. The leader will describe a sharp curve and follow after, and will not be seen by the fish before he sees the fly. After the fly has alighted, the rod should be held consistently pointed directly at the fly and in a horizontal position. Held in this way, it is less likely to be seen by the fish and a better control of the line is had if a rise be effected.

There are, in fact, good reasons why the rod should be held horizontally whenever and wherever the floating fly is being used, the line being stripped in by the unoccupied hand as much as may be necessary to keep the fly under control.

If the current be rapid between the angler and the fish, he should use a foot or two more of line and try to throw a larger curve in the leader so that the fly may reach the fish before drag is exerted upon it. If the cast be well done there is at least an even chance that the fly will be taken; if not well done, no move should be made to retrieve the fly until it has floated some distance below the fish, and even then the retrieve should not be made directly from the water with the full length of line. The line, leader, and fly will be swept down-stream at a speed depending upon the current, and will be approaching the angler's bank. By stripping the line in slowly and carefully, the fly may be lightly whisked off with little or no disturbance of the surface when there is little but the leader upon the water, and another attempt made. The angler may continue this process as long as he feels he has made no mistake.

If the fly has been refused after a number of casts, and the fish continues to rise, it is some consolation to know that he has not been disturbed by the casting. A change of tactics is very often effective in such cases; and, if the fly be placed very close to the fish instead of being floated down to him, its sudden appearance, giving but little time for investigation, may cause him to rise to it.

When a rising fish may be cast to without disturbing those below him, the angler is in a more favourable position. Where practicable, the effort should be to make the throw with the leader curved and above the fly. Naturally, this is more easily accomplished when the fish—looking up-stream—is on the angler's left hand. Unless one be ambidextrous, or skilful enough to throw with the right hand from over the left shoulder, a fish under the right-hand bank is difficult to reach in this manner. Until the cast has been mastered, no attempt should be made to throw the curve; but one need not despair of taking fish in this position, even though this skill be lacking. The fly may be thrown straight, but from a more obtuse angle; and if, instead of being placed directly over or above the fish, it be placed slightly above and a foot to the near side of the spot where he rose, the danger of scaring him off with the leader is lessened, and the chance of his taking it not a bit.

Where a long cast is required, the line should never be extended to the length required to reach the fish. The distance should be measured carefully, and, when the fly in the false or air casts reaches a point five or six feet from the fish, that much line—which should be stripped from the reel and held in the left hand—should be allowed to pass through the guides on the next forward cast. This is called shooting the line. Not only is it of great assistance in attaining accuracy, but the momentum imparted to the "live" line, that part already clear of the top, is lost and does not travel down to the fly, which, shorn of impulse, remains suspended for an instant above the water and falls thereon as lightly as the proverbial feather.

The fly should never be aimed directly at the water, but at an imaginary point three or four feet above, and a like distance in advance of, the spot it is desired to reach. This direction must be implicitly observed in this method of casting, because the fly will invariably fall short unless a greater length of line be used than is apparently necessary. Very often the fly will fall heavily if just the required length of line is used without "shooting."

Where a fish is rising in the strong current, a short line, not over twenty-five feet, will be sufficient and quite enough to handle, as it is returned very quickly to the angler. In this case the "shoot" may be abandoned in the actual delivery of the fly and used only to lengthen the line between casts after the retrieve, which should be made only when the fly has passed considerably behind the fish—the exact distance naturally being determined by the circumstances. The line should be stripped with the left hand to keep pace with the speed with which the fly travels and no faster, else its action will not be natural.

Nothing but the fly and leader should be on the water, and as little of the latter as possible. Get behind the fish, but do not cast directly over him. The fly should come down past him to one side or the other, with the leader always on the same side—away from the fish.

Early in the season, if the weather be propitious and the stream in good condition, it is not unlikely that fish will be seen rising throughout the day—perhaps not all of the time but often enough to keep the angler alert. The fact that they are rising at all is quite sufficient to arouse his interest, because, even though the fish nearest him does not take his fly, the one above may; and, all things considered, he may hope to have a fairly interesting day, with the further chance, if fortune smiles, of a good one.

How different the situation confronting the angler who elects to fish the streams in the hot summer months, with the water at its lowest mark, clear as crystal—or gin, as the Englishman has it—and not a fish to be seen rising the whole livelong day, for the very good reason that no insects are about to offer inducement. Even in June these conditions sometimes prevail, with the redeeming feature, however, that toward evening the falling temperature, or the approach of darkness, or both, seem to induce a rise of insects, with an accompanying rise of trout. The angler, having patiently waited for this time, sets hard at work and is content to take a couple of fair fish in the hour or so before dark.

I confess to a certain weakness for the stream during those periods of extreme heat when the local experts agree that it is almost impossible to take fish. Actuated, perhaps, as much by a desire to take a good fish as by the hope of learning whether or not their theories were correct, I have gone to the stream under such conditions and have had some curious experiences. I have taken fine fish on broiling hot days when there seemed to be little difference between the temperature of the water and the air. On days when the "hatch" has been so thin that one would be warranted in thinking that the trout had forgotten that there ever was such a thing as a fly, I have taken some of my best fish. On the other hand, there have been many occasions when I have met with utter defeat, and, all in all, I hardly know what I have really learned from the experiences, so varied have they been.

One insufferably hot July day convinced me, however, that there are times when trout are interested neither in food nor in anything else. For three sultry hours I cast over every likely spot. I never rose a fish. I never saw one rise. I did not see a fish.

At a beautiful pool, small but of good depth, considering the state of the water, I felt that my last chance had come, and after covering the whole surface carefully, without result, deliberately waded into it, hoping to scare any fish that might be there and so learn where they were hiding. I did not see a fin, and had about decided it was tenantless, when, looking down, I saw, close to my feet, the tail of a fish sticking out from under a small boulder. I looked under the up-stream side of the boulder, hoping to see the fish's head, but could not, as there was no hollow on that side. I gently stroked that part of the fish in sight with the tip of my rod, and received in acknowledgment a gentle waving of the tail. Placing my gear behind me in the dry bed of the stream, I proceeded to move the boulder to see what manner of trout this might be. Not until I had it completely removed did he stir—and then he moved but a short distance to a similar hiding-place. He was a brown trout about fifteen inches long, and so sluggish was he that it would have been the simplest matter to have seized him with my hands.

A short distance above the pool there is a dam famous for the big trout which make their home under it. I covered the water faithfully, without success, and, after I had finished, crawled out upon the apron of the dam. Peering into the pool below, I saw, directly underneath me, eighteen or twenty trout ranging from six inches in length to one old "lunker" over twenty. As this spot had been cast over repeatedly, and apparently without any glaring error, I felt in no humour to try again, but determined to test their appetites in another way. Catching a half dozen grasshoppers, I dropped one in front of the big fish that led the school. He paid not the slightest attention to it. Neither did any of the others, not even the smallest one. I tried again, throwing another grasshopper a bit upstream so that it would float down in plain view for a long time, and again provoked no interest upon the part of the fish. Finally, I killed one of the grasshoppers, crushing it so that it would sink, and threw it well above the fish. It came down under water directly on a line with the big fish, which deliberately moved a bit to one side, apparently to avoid having it touch him. Each fish behind him did the same thing, even the smallest ones ignoring it.

Now, what sort of a fly, wet, sunk, or dry, or, if the angler was inclined to try it, what sort of bait could he use to interest such fish? Under the conditions then prevailing —the thermometer recording 94 degrees in the shade, the stream at its lowest point, and the temperature of the water very high—I really believe that the only chance he might have had would have been with a very "wet" mint julep. Under the circumstances it would have required considerable self-denial to have offered that. This heat was exceptional, however, and fishing in such weather is quite as trying as fishing in the cold, blustering days of early spring. In either case, even if fish are taken, enthusiasm is not greatly aroused on the part of either angler or trout.

I confess I do not know what method of fly fishing one may use to entice a trout when the temperature is extreme, because when the fish is found under a boulder, as he probably will be, he will not see a floating fly, and it is almost hopeless to expect a sunken fly to attract any attention— witness the case of the idle fish and the grasshoppers. If fish not hiding in caverns refuse live grasshoppers dropped directly in front of their noses, it is quite evident that there is small chance of taking them on any sort of artificial lure.

Leaving out of consideration, however, the few periods of unbearable heat, that part of the season between June 15 and August 31 may have many days rich in experience for the angler, and even though there be many days when the fish will be found not to be rising to natural insects, the pleasure derivable from trying for success is commensurate with the difficulty of approaching and luring them.

When the streams are low and clear great circumspection and care are required in approaching fish or likely places and in presenting the fly. The slightest error will be detected at once, and subsequent attempts to interest the fish will be effort merely wasted.

The angler who carefully casts over and thoroughly fishes a likely piece of water should not come too quickly to the conclusion that it contains no fish. If it happens to be one of those days (too frequent in the experience of the present-day angler) when a great length of stream may be traversed without his seeing the slightest indication of a rising fish, he may, of course, if he be so inclined, comfort himself with the thought that the fish are not feeding and abandon his fishing. But I hope to show that upon just such days the proper use of the dry fly will measure the difference between an empty creel and some success, even though that success be limited to the probability of a single good fish.

An English dry fly angler fishing our Eastern American streams by rote and casting only over or to rising fish would have many empty days to record in his diary. Days and days might pass without his seeing the "dimple" of a big fish or even the splash of a small one, except, possibly, just at dusk; and at such times his skill and patience would be taxed as heavily as ever by any smutting fish of a chalk stream. But does it follow, as some authorities seem to have suggested, that because a fish is not risen by a few casts here and there it has no inclination to come to the surface or that such inclination may not be aroused? I think not, my experience having proven the contrary.

The entire theory of forcing the fish to rise to the fly is

based upon the fact that a trout may be decoyed from the position occupied by it when not feeding to one fixed by the angler, provided, of course, the fish is not asked to come any great distance. The practice of the method necessitates considerable knowledge of the fish and of the character of the places it frequents. The fly cast, say, twenty times, in close proximity to the supposed lair of a fish, in nine cases out of ten will prove more effective than twice the same number of casts placed indiscriminately over the water. But no glaring mistake, such as undue splashing or frantic waving of the rod, is overlooked by the fish. If such errors have been committed, the angler had best retire and try some fish that has not become acquainted with him.

Having chosen the point of vantage from which to assail the fish, which choice should be governed, first, by reason of its being out of range of the trout's vision, and then by the availability of casting room behind—note the order of importance—the single fly should be placed a foot or two from the spot where the fish is supposed to be and to one side of it. The instructions given in regard to casting to bulging fish so as to produce the effect of a hatch should be followed to the letter. Even where the distance seems rather too far to expect the fish to travel, it is better to select water that flows continuously in one direction in which to place the fly. It is preferable to have the fly travel in one "lane" during its promenade, rather than to have its action marred by a possible drag resulting from an attempt to get it closer to the fish. If the fly has been natural in its action, it is quite likely that it has attracted the attention

of the fish, and the angler may at any moment be amazed
to see a trout backing slowly down-stream under it, seemingly coming from nowhere. This is the trying time, as the
fish, having come closer to the angler, is more likely to be
frightened off by any sudden movement; but if the angler
is careful, the satisfaction of eventually seeing the fish rise
deliberately and fasten to the fly is not to be measured by
that of taking a larger fish by any other method.

Great care should be exercised in retrieving the fly from
the water, because a fish taking up a position under the
angler's lane of flies usually backs down-stream a bit. In
no case should the fly be retrieved until it has floated down
to a point nearly at right angles to or even below the rod.
Strict observance of this rule will prevent scaring off many
fish that might otherwise be induced to rise.

Where the swiftness of the current precludes any possibility of preventing drag, particularly in those miniature
pools behind rocks in the centre of the stream called
"pockets," the fly may be placed lightly thereon, and as
lightly whisked away, being left but an instant, to be returned immediately and often, until the angler is satisfied
that the pocket contains no fish, or that he is unable to interest them if it does. In any event, he need not feel that
an opportunity has been lost to him because of his inability
to avoid drag, for in this sort of water the error is not
always observed by the fish.

There can be no question but that stalking a feeding
fish and finally taking him on an artificial fly affords sport
of the highest quality. The taking of a fish that may be

seen but is not feeding, either because of lack of food or disinclination, is quite as difficult to accomplish, however, and is productive of equally good sport.

I relate the following story of the taking of a trout under almost impossible conditions, not so much to illustrate the success of the method as to show the satisfaction that attends the accomplishment of the feat. This individual fish is only one of many that I have taken similarly in the many years that I have fished with the floating fly, and the history of its taking is given here because it illustrates and bolsters up my claim that the dry fly repeatedly cast over a sluggish, non-feeding fish will induce him to rise.

The last two days of the season of 1909, August 29 and 30, found me on the banks of the Kaaterskill, at Palenville, Greene County, N. Y. This stream is a brawling one, resembling many Rocky Mountain streams, and some magnificent rainbow trout inhabit it; yet in six hours' fishing, one afternoon, I raised but one good-sized fish, in which I left my fly. The dozen or more fish from ten to twenty inches in length which could be seen restlessly swimming about in each of the pools appeared to be interested in nothing but a desire to escape the intense heat, and at length I abandoned the sport as hopeless.

A gentleman who had once lived in that section, and who had fished the streams of the surrounding country for over thirty years, invited me to fish a stream some miles away with him the next day. I accepted his invitation, and the morning found us on the banks of what should have been the Plattekill, but proved to be nothing but a mere

trickle. With many misgivings I started in, my companion
going up-stream about a mile to fish down and meet me.

The only likely water within three or four hundred yards
was a pool under a dam, and here I rose and pricked a
good fish. Leaving him, I cut across a neck of land to meet
my companion at the turn, and found him ready to quit.
But I determined to try again for the fish I had risen, and,
while following the stream back, discovered a pool against
the bank, some eight feet wide and not over a dozen in
length, with six feet of water in it. On the bottom lay a fine
brown trout, as motionless as if dead. He was actually lying
on the sand and pebbles, apparently devoid of all interest
in life. I withdrew quietly and, getting below him and behind a tree-stump on the bank, put on a new fly—a Whirling Dun—and, with but little hope, sent the fly on its
errand. It fell lightly upon the glassy surface about a yard
above the fish, which was at all times in plain view; but
he seemed entirely oblivious to it. There was practically
no current to carry it down, and it seemed an interminable
length of time before the fly got below the fish far enough
for me to take it off the water without disturbance; but
at last I retrieved it and, after drying it thoroughly,
dropped it again. I repeated this operation six times before
I noticed any change in the position of the fish, and all of
the time he was just "lolling" on the bottom. The sixth
cast seemed to attract his attention, and, with all fins
moving, he lifted ever so little from the bottom and stood
poised. I felt that I had him interested—that he was alert—
and I knew that the slightest mistake from then on meant
failure, complete and certain; and my excitement was not

helping a bit. Another cast, and I imagined I could see him tremble; at any rate, his fins moved rapidly, but without imparting any motion to the body, except to lift it an inch or two toward the surface. Each succeeding cast brought the same excited action of the fins and tempted him a few inches nearer the surface. I thought he never would reach the top, and felt that if he didn't get within his distance soon I would bungle the whole affair. At last, and after I had made more than twenty-five casts, he had risen to within six inches of the surface; as the fly was presented again, he made a determined rush, stopping just short of it and allowing it to float over him, apparently without further interest. I gently retrieved the fly, though I felt that it was all over, as the fish had probably detected the fraud. However, I made another cast and the fly fortunately alighted softly. The fish made the same rush, refusing it as before; but after the fly had floated down a foot or so, he turned slowly and deliberately down-stream, and, rising quietly, took the fly with a distinct "suck," turned to go down with it, and was fast.

This was not a very large trout—fifteen inches or so—but his taking afforded more genuine sport than a dozen larger ones might have yielded taken in any other way, because of the circumstances under which it was accomplished. I may have had a possible advantage over him, because a floating fly had, probably, never been cast on the stream before. Aside from this fact, it cannot be said that the element of luck entered into the affair at all, except, perhaps, in so far as it enabled me to deliver my fly so many times without mistake. I have, however, taken many other and larger fish in practically the same manner and by the employment of the same tactics, and know the method to be sound in theory and practice. For the solace of the beginner who may attempt to practise the method, let me add that in the beginning the fish I took were, probably, a very small number of those from which all thoughts of feeding were driven by my bungling.

If a trout lying in a small pool and in plain view, as was the one whose story has just been told, could be induced to come up through six feet of water to take the fly, is it not fair to assume that an unseen fish may also be forced to rise by the same tactics? Of course, in the case of an unseen fish, the angler labours under some disadvantage, because he is casting somewhat in the dark. In addition to ability to deliver many casts perfectly to a selected spot, he must also have the experience and knowledge that enable him to decide, at least approximately, where the fish may lie under the prevailing conditions. If his judgment in this particular is at fault his chances of rising the fish are gone. He should, therefore, assume that it occupies any of three or four positions, and for his first cast should choose that one of them which may be cast over with the least danger of disturbing the fish should it occupy any one of the others. If a rise be not had after a certain number of casts over the chosen position, the others should each be fished in turn.

The chance of putting down a fish for good will increase in proportion to the number of casts over each position, multiplied by the number of positions. That a rise is not had from the position first chosen will not prove that a fish does not occupy it, and the angler's subsequent casts will be made under increased difficulty, because of his efforts to refrain from further disturbing that water.

Before leaving this subject, and at the risk of becoming somewhat tedious and tiring my reader, I will relate the circumstances of the taking of an unseen fish by repeatedly casting over a chosen spot—in other words, of "forcing a rise." The incident has an added interest because a fellow angler witnessed it and was thereby convinced that a fish could be moved into position by the fly.

We were fishing the Brodhead, in Pennsylvania. It was in July and the day was very hot. The water was extremely low and very clear, and the upper reach of the stream just below the Canadensis bridge, which we had elected to fish, did not look big enough to hold a trout of any size. In one particular stretch there was a hundred yards of very shallow water, a small pocket on the right-hand bank being the only likely looking spot. I knew this stretch held many fine fish when the stream was in better condition, and I decided that this particular pocket might be the abiding-place of a good trout. As it was approaching the noon hour, I determined to go no farther up-stream but to spend a half hour experimenting on the little pocket.

The surface of the miniature pool was not ever eight feet wide anywhere nor more than that in length, but its depth below a jutting rock which formed one side of it convinced me that it was worth trying, although there was no actual indication that a fish occupied it. The bottom was plainly discernible except in the swifter water near the head, and, as no fish could be seen, I selected the edge of this swift water upon which to place my fly. A dozen or more casts were made without any apparent effect, when suddenly a yellow gleam at the tail of the pocket, just after the fly had floated over the lip, disclosed a fine trout poised in the flattening water. Explaining the situation to my companion—who was now all excitement, having seen the fish, and who really did not believe it could be taken—on the spur of the moment I decided to try to prove my theory at the risk of losing the fish. I ceased casting to him. We watched him for probably two or three minutes, during which time he appeared to be keenly alert, when he quietly left his position and moved back up-stream into the swift water and out of sight. My opportunity had come, although my friend thought I had lost it. To make more certain that the colour of the fly played no part in the affair, I substituted a Silver Sedge for the Whirling Dun I had been using. After about a dozen casts with this fly there came the same yellow gleam, and the fish was back into position again. This time I continued casting, and, although he seemed to "lean" toward the fly each time it came down, he did not take it until it had passed by ten times, finally rising deliberately and fastening on the eleventh cast. He proved to weigh one pound ten ounces.

To what conclusion does the observation of this fish bring us? If he had been ready to feed before the artificial appeared, is it likely that he would have permitted it to pass over or near him a score of times before taking? And when he occupied what I call his feeding position, why did he allow the fly to pass ten times although exhibiting a certain interest in it each time? It was never beyond his reach and could easily have been taken. Was the desire to feed being gradually aroused in him at each sight of the fly? When he did take it, it was done with such certainty that he must have believed it to be a natural, although quite unlike anything he had recently seen. One thing is certain, however. He was decoyed from one position to another on two occasions within a few minutes of each other, and by a different pattern of fly each time.

CHAPTER IV
WHERE AND WHEN TO FISH

T HE swift streams in the eastern part of the United States must, as a rule, be fished by wading. Where it is possible, because of the absence of trees and brush, to fish from the bank, the angler's form is silhouetted sharply against the background of sky, and, to overcome this disadvantage, he must retire some distance from the edge of the bank, or, if he wishes to come closer, must kneel or crouch to avoid being seen by the fish. By casting from the bank he will avoid the disturbance of the water necessarily made by entering it, and this is, of course, an advantage. On the other hand, he is closer to the surface of the stream while wading, in which position he is not so easily seen, which is also an advantage. Offsetting the latter, however, is the commotion made by his movements, which, no matter how deliberate, will make the trout nervous or apprehensive of approaching danger. If he has shown himself, even though the fish has been vigorously feeding, he might just as well abandon any attempt to induce a rise, because the trout, having been warned by his careless approach, will have scurried away. The danger of putting down a fish in swift water is not so great because the ripples sent in advance of the angler make little headway and travel no great distance against a strong current.

To describe places where trout may be looked for under any and all circumstances, is practically impossible. Very often the fish will not be found where the angler thinks they should be. They are as full of notions and idiosyncrasies as anglers themselves, and one may hope to become familiar with their habitat in a general way only, and this after close study. I say "in a general way," because, while a big trout may be known to inhabit a certain pool, it does not follow that he is in the same spot today that he occupied yesterday or the day before. He may be looked for somewhere about, but a distance of even three or four feet from his previous known position may so place him as to prevent the angler from approaching without being seen. I am speaking of fish that are not rising. Of course, if they should be feeding upon the surface they are easily spotted.

Each pool or piece of water should be examined carefully after it has been fished. In this way the deeper holes, the nooks under the banks, and the crevices between boulders are discovered and marked down. If the angler is to spend much time on a stream that is new to him, it is even permissible to enter the deeper water quietly for the purpose of a thorough investigation; but under no circumstances should this be done if other anglers are upon the stream. As a rule, we are too careless of others' rights, and the ethics of fly fishing should be observed quite as closely as the code that governs our actions in any other sport.

A long, flat stretch of the stream is likely to contain many big fish, and must be approached in the most circumspect manner. The angler who hopes to take one of them should study the water carefully before entering it, and strive to determine just where the biggest fish lie. The character of the water and its temperature and the prevailing weather conditions are the data from which he must make his deductions.

By way of illustration, let us assume that the angler is upon the stream, prepared to fish it.

The day is one somewhere between the first of May and the fifteenth of June. It is not too bright, and a light wind with a touch of summer in it is blowing up-stream. The water is running down after a light rain, and while not crystal clear is not much discoloured. It is about five-thirty o'clock of the afternoon, and the trout from below the stretch are coming on the feed. The flat to be fished is about one hundred and fifty feet long from where the water flows into it to where it rolls out again at the tail, and about fifty feet wide where the banks are farthest apart, narrowing, fan-like, to ten feet or less at the head. The current, gliding silently along the left bank (looking up-stream), shows the deep water to be on that side. These are ideal conditions, of course, and I have chosen them for that very reason. The angler is indeed fortunate who happens upon the stream when they prevail.

The natural place to look for trout under such conditions is anywhere along the left bank in the deep water. If flies are hatching—as in all probability they will be at this season—the angler need but watch for the rise that will indicate the position of the feeding fish. If these fish be small, as will be evidenced by the "staccato smack" made as the fly is taken, he should move farther up-stream, because no really big feeding fish need be looked for where small ones are: *vice versa*, little fish rarely feed in the same place and at the same time as big ones. If no rise is seen, the task then is to locate the fish, and, under the favourable conditions prevailing, it may be fairly assumed that they are ready to feed. There will be one place in the flat where more surface food collects than in any other, and one place where more comes down-stream because of converging currents. In one of such places the biggest fish will be found.

Wherever an eddy swirls gently against a small cove in the bank, or the force of the current spends itself against a rock, making a dead water or backwater above it, the fly may search and find many fine trout. If the backwater at the head of the stretch is of an area great enough to collect and hold the foam made by the tumbling water, this is the spot from which the angler may hope to secure one of the best fish in the pool, if not *the* best. One of the favourite feeding positions of a large trout is under this foam, and the fly, placed carefully again and again, often tempts him to move into his feeding position when, at the beginning of the casting, he lay outside of it. The fly should be dropped lightly on the foam and permitted to remain there until it is snatched away by the current.

It may happen that this particular part of the stretch does not contain one very large fish that "lords it" over a considerable area, but a number of fair-sized ones which, if feeding, will be somewhat scattered, and should be looked for in each of the places described.

Before or after the foam, backwater, and eddies have been tried, preferably before, the water on either side of the swiftest part of the current should be cast over, the fly being placed just at the bottom and at the side of the "lumpy" water. A fly cast to this position is extremely effective, dancing most naturally as it comes swiftly downstream. This water should be tested thoroughly, the fly being placed always in the same spot and permitted to follow the same course for as long a distance as possible.

As daylight wanes, the fish often drop back to the tail of the stretch, sometimes feeding upon the very lip, or just above where the water begins to quicken before it spills out. This habit of trout may be due to their becoming less wary as dark approaches, and, consequently, quite willing to enter shallower water, where they find it easier to pick up a few insects or a minnow or two than in the deeper, swifter water above. Wherefore, if the angler has been unsuccessful at the head of the stretch, let him, by travelling circuitously, find a position some distance below the lip, and fish the still water carefully as long as he can see his fly.

If the day is hot and bright, the water low and clear, and the fish not in any of the positions already described, they may be in either one of two places—along the bank or in the white water at the head.

If the fish are lying alongside of the bank they will prove to be as difficult to take as the most fastidious could wish. Knowledge of the crannies, depth, etc., will help the angler and make his task easier. But if the water is strange to him, and the trout must be searched for, his task is more complicated and he must exercise the greatest care in approaching. In many cases the stretches are lined on both sides by alders, willows, and the like, that make it impossible to cast without entering the water and, by so doing, forming ripples which, advancing ahead of the fly, warn the trout that danger is afoot. Exercising patience, he may walk slowly and quietly into the water at the tail of the stretch and as closely as possible to the bank the fish are under. Having attained the desired position, he should remain there long enough to allow all commotion made by his entry to cease, during which time no motion of the rod should be made, because the sight of any moving object will send the now alert trout scurrying, while the ripples will make him uneasy for a short time only. The horizontal cast should be used if possible. The fly should be floated down about a foot from the bank, and it should not be retrieved until it has travelled more than half the distance between the angler and the spot where it alighted. Casting should be continued until a mistake has marred the attempt, when the angler should desist, to resume after a short time has elapsed if the error has not been a glaring one.

When satisfied that no trout are within the section covered by the fly, the angler should lengthen his line and fish the fly a few feet above—always permitting the fly to travel over the water already fished. He should continue this until the maximum line that can be handled neatly without moving from the original position is being cast. When the line becomes unwieldy (in this method and position it is courting failure to attempt anything over thirty-five to forty feet, even if one is expert) an advance may be made a few yards up-stream as closely to the bank as the depth of the water and free casting space will permit. As it is quite possible—and likely, too—that a trout has been under the fly all the while, but was not interested in it, the angler's advance will drive him ahead, and indications of this should be sharply looked for. The discovery of the fish will save much valuable time, for in that case the immediate stretch may be abandoned, because any fish above the one seen will have certainly taken alarm at the actions of his fellow and will have lost all desire to feed for some time.

If no fish is disturbed, search the bank carefully along its length, always remembering to have the fly float down a considerable distance before retrieving. The chances are quite even, if the approach has been made carefully and quietly, that a good fish will be risen. In such water only skill of the highest type is rewarded. If it is not possible to follow along the bank under which the trout are lying, the cast may be made from the opposite side; but in this case a longer line should be used. If the water must be entered to reach the bank from the opposite side—and this, unfortunately, is usually the case—the angler should not move or allow his rod to move for some time after he has taken his position.

Having reached the head of the stretch, the angler may go over the eddies, backwater, and swift, and, if he meets with no response, the white water. This, above all places, is the diffiicult water to fish with the dry fly, and many anglers believe it to be quite impossible. If the dry fly be fished as is the wet fly—that is, cast in the swirl and allowed to drift about and down—it will become thoroughly drenched. But if it is placed properly and with due calculation, it is as easily kept dry and floating as upon any other part of the stream. The explanation lies in the fact that the fly is not placed directly upon the white water at all, if it be properly placed, but is cast to either side of the swift water, always on the side nearest the angler first, who should pick out the smooth looking spots upon which to place the fly. The fish which the wet fly angler takes directly from the centre of the current are taken on the dry fly by being induced to move out of their position. A very short line is used, and the fly is floated but a foot or two, being dropped lightly again and again. I will admit that trout are not taken from the white water in this way by the dry fly as frequently as they are with the sunk fly, but when one *is* taken it is usually a good fish.

On either side of the brink of the miniature fall above the white water may be seen boulders, seemingly acting as gatemen, directing the running waters to pass between. The current gliding swiftly toward them, deflected to right and left, reminds one of a flock of sheep all trying to get through a gap in the fence at the same time, those caught against the edge of the opening making little headway; and so it is with that part of the current which spends most of its force against the boulders. If this water be examined it will be discovered that considerable dead or back water is formed under the surface just above the boulders. Such places are among the selected retreats of *Salmo fario*.

A fly floated down from a point two feet above and retrieved just as it is about to go over the fall may produce a very pretty picture for the angler. If the fly upon its first appearance has been seen by the trout, he is often induced to rush at it, and, missing, goes headlong over the fall, instinct telling him, perhaps, that he may find it below. Not to disappoint him, the angler drops it immediately at the edge of the white water, where it usually meets with a vicious reception. Should all not come off as planned, the fly may be cast again above the boulder and retrieved as before. The fish may be tempted to dart out and seize it after a dozen or more casts. If hooked, he will come over the fall to be dealt with in the smoother water below, and the angler will not have missed the picture, after all.

Native trout rarely occupy such positions, but they should never be overlooked in streams known to contain brown or rainbow trout.

Sometimes a short stretch of smooth, swift water will be found sweeping silently along the mossy bank just above the sentinel boulders at the head of the white water. The bank is probably shaded by overhanging rhododendron, or alder growth, that lends to the water a peculiar greenish hue. This stretch may be occupied by fine fish that, because of some effect of light or shade, seem better able to detect the approach of an angler or the connection of the leader with the fly than do fish in similar waters unshaded. A longer line is necessary here, and great care should be exercised to refrain, as far as possible, from entering that arc of a circle which is presumed to limit the range of the trout's vision. Difficulty will also be experienced in handling the line, owing to the greater length used and the rapidity with which it will be returned by the current. The danger of scaring the fish is minimized if the fly be delivered from a point almost directly in line with the current and the horizontal cast used. While not always necessary, the horizontal cast is better at all times, as the fly seems to cock more readily when thrown from this angle.

As a stretch of this character is usually of uniform depth along the greater part of its length, the fish may be in any part of it on a "feeding" day—a day when those below seemed to have been willing to feed. The fly should be placed at the foot of the stretch and on the side nearest the rod, and gradually worked, in the subsequent casts, toward the centre and head. This must be done slowly, however, and the fly should not be retrieved until it has come down some distance and has passed the spot where the first cast was delivered. The fish, in all probability, will be found near the middle of the stretch and to the side of the centre of the current nearer the bank. No attempt should be made to get closer, because the chance of having the fish come to the fly is greater than that of his taking after the line has been seen.

When the prevailing conditions indicate that the trout are not in the open—in other words, are not fully engaged in feeding or in looking for food—they will usually be found lying near the bank. In such cases, the first attempt should be made at the tail or down-stream end of the swift, the fly being gradually worked up-stream a foot or so at a time and about a foot from the bank. It should be allowed to drift down to the foot of the stretch each time, and the casting continued until the entire length of the bank has been thoroughly searched. If the bank should be of gravelly or earthy formation it may be an overhanging one, having been undermined by the action of the current. The angler may be certain that this is so if that part above water shows a mass or network of bared roots. In this case the same procedure is followed, with the exception that the fly should be placed two feet, or even more, from the edge of the tangle, so that it may come the better within the angle of the fish's vision. It is quite obvious that a fly placed too close to the bank will be unseen by a fish occupying the hollow under it. Great perseverance, even persistence, is required to induce a fish to leave a retreat of this sort in which he is snugly ensconced, but the attempt should not be abandoned while it is certain that no blunder has been made. Large trout love these places, and coaxing one out is worth a great deal of effort.

Long before a rise is effected, warning of the possibility of its coming off is given by the flash of a trout as he leaves his position under the bank to assume another under the lane or *hatch* of frauds. The trout is often a better judge of distance than the angler, and when this action of the fish is observed, any attempt to make it easier for him by placing the fly closer to the bank will, in all probability, put a stop to further interest on his part. Difficult as it is to disobey the impulse to place the fly where the fish was seen, it must be resisted, because, while there is a possibility that the fish may be risen, there is a greater likelihood that he will be put down. For this reason the original plan should be followed without deviation. Ask him to come to the fly, and, while he may seem diffident at first, he will finally accept the invitation.

These swifts, or runs, as they are termed, vary in length from fifteen to fifty feet, or more, and the greater their length the more difficult they are for the angler to cover without showing himself. They are the narrows of the stream, and, where the water is found to be of unvarying depth, the fish may be looked for in any part of them. The steady, rapid flow of the current is admirably adapted to the use of the floating fly, and is particularly attractive to those impatient ones who are unwilling to wait and watch the fly's slow progress on the quieter waters. Where the run being fished is distinctly "lumpy"—that is, where its speed is greater because of the sharper incline in the stream bed, and miniature waves are formed that hurry down one after another—the floating fly will be more difficult to handle, but is very effective if well placed.

It was once my good fortune to see a stretch of this character on the Neversink fished by a friend, Mr. Walter McGuckin, who has been my companion on many fishing excursions. He is one of the best hands with a rod that I have ever seen. His precision with the fly is remarkable, and I doubt if the grace and ease with which he handles his line can be excelled. His skill is fortified with a knowledge of trout gained by over thirty-five years' experience on the waters of New York State. And, by the by, although he has used the wet fly for the greater portion of this time, he will now take his fish on the dry fly or not at all.

The weather of four seasons had been crowded into a

single day—and this at the end of May. Although no insects of any kind had been seen, we had been able to mark
a fish down the day before, when he had shown himself
for an instant. Having fished the smooth water on either
side of the centre of the current without engaging the fish's
attention, my friend decided to "ride his fly" on top of the
waves in the very swiftest part of the current. To do this
effectively, and without having too much of the leader on
the water, the chance of exposing himself to the fish was
taken, as the fly had to be delivered from almost a right
angle. However, it all came off correctly, and the fly,
seeming barely to touch the water as it danced along,
appeared even more lifelike than a natural insect. So, too,
it must have appeared to the trout, for, after a number of
casts had been made, a fish leaped directly from one wave
to the one above, upon which was the fly, took it with
mouth wide open and dived under. He was led gently to
the still water below, and, although he proved to be a fine
brown trout, his manner of taking the fly appealed to us
more than his quality, and he was returned to the stream.
The rise is the thing, and a dashing one of this sort makes
the blood quicken as the dull *chug* of a fish taking under
water never can.

When a trout is taken on a floating fly from beneath the
tangled rubbish which collects about the submerged roots
of a fallen tree or stump, the angler may attribute his success to common sense and reason more than to his dexterity in placing the fly. If we assume that the fish is under
the tangle, taking advantage of the shade and protection it
affords, is it logical to expect him to worm his way up

through it to take a fly? And, as his head is invariably pointed up-stream, is it at all likely that a fly placed behind him will be observed? The answer is obviously, no! When a trout occupies a position of this character, it is always because of its proximity to water which will permit him the greatest freedom in securing food or in escaping from danger. He is often unwilling, and frequently unable, to dart rapidly down-stream when moved by either of these considerations, and the fly should be so presented that it will ask nothing uncommon of him.

Many anglers fail to take fish from these justly famed and wisely chosen domiciles of big trout, because of their reluctance or inability to estimate the odds on or against the sporting proposition. They are not ready to risk a ten cent fly for the purpose of properly fishing a spot which has cost them a hundred times as much to reach. With a few desultory casts—placed, usually, where they will do the least good and where, perhaps, a dozen others have been placed before that same day, sometimes within the hour—they move on. Congratulating themselves that they are safely out of a tight place, or comforting themselves with the thought that if a trout had been hooked it would have been lost anyway in the tangled mass, they abandon the spot—but always, I opine, with a lingering look backward. That these promising but difficult waters are prone to lure the angler into danger of hanging up solidly should make them the more interesting. When a good trout is taken from them, it is usually by a master of the craft, and no compassion need be wasted upon the fish—it has fallen into good and deserving hands.

The common practice of careless anglers is to place the fly as close to the root or snag as they can, where there is but slight chance of its being seen by the fish—at least while it is upon the surface. Naturally, if the fly be sunk to a depth which will bring it within the horizontal plane of the fish's vision, it will be seen by him more readily. But in fishing the floating fly, due allowance must be made for that portion of an imaginary circle enclosing the base of an inverted cone which will not come within view of the fish at the apex. This part will be directly over him, extending at an angle measured by the diameter of the root or snag under which he is hiding, this snag and the bank naturally being included in the calculation. To reach a fish in this position, or rather to place the fly so that it will be seen by him, an imaginary semicircle should be drawn about the spot, with a diameter equal to at least twice the known diameter of the obstacle, and the fly fished on this curved line until the circumference has been covered. Unless the angler can determine accurately the depth of the water or the submerged portion of the log, root, or whatever the obstacle may be, any allowance made over and above what appears necessary from the calculation will be to his advantage.

The down-stream part of the imaginary semicircle will prove to be the least productive, for the reason that it is difficult to interest a fish from behind, he being more concerned about happenings in front of him. Nevertheless, considerable effort should be expended upon this part of it, as there is always a possibility of the fish being nearer the angler than has been calculated. Having fished it thoroughly, the water along the upper half of it may then be covered. The edge of this segment of the semicircle should be reached from a point nearly at right angles to its tangent, the angler retiring and assuming a position at a reasonable distance from the point being assailed. The rise may be looked for in that water where the swiftest part of the current flows directly toward and against the obstruction. And, as it is advantageous to have the fly cover a great distance upon the surface, it should be dropped a foot or two farther up-stream from the snag than when casting to the side of it. If the flow against the obstruction be studied there will be discovered on the edge of the current nearest the angler a spot whence the fly, being placed correctly, will be carried down to the obstacle and around it and will thus be exposed to the view of the trout without danger of drag or of "hanging up." The fly alone must travel in this part of the current, and the longer it travels in sight of the fish the greater is the likelihood of interesting him. Barring, always, the chance of error, the probability of taking the fish increases with each cast made. The situation confronting the angler who fastens to a fish in this water is a very trying one, and, if a fish so hooked is to be saved for the creel, tender methods will not avail. He must be unceremoniously bundled out and away from the dangerous spot, with every turn and crook of which he is familiar.

Aside from the fact that fishing well out from an obstacle gives a fish beneath it a more certain chance of seeing the angler's fly, the method has an additional advantage in that it lessens the risk of "hanging up" on one of the early casts—an accident that is very apt to cut short the angler's attempt if he tries to deliver his fly in places that are difficult to reach. But the angler who is unwilling to chance the loss of a fly by placing it close to a mass of drift or overhanging branches is not over-anxious to take sizable fish, and his success is usually meagre, in proportion to the risk assumed.

Fishing the "edge of the circle" will frequently be found to be more effective than the accepted practice of searching the intricate tangles and openings, and is advocated as supplemental thereto.

A rift, properly speaking, is a shallow part of the stream where the current is quite rapid and more or less broken, and may be from ten yards in length to a mile or more. Where such water is spread from bank to bank and is very shallow, with but slight change in depth, little sport may be looked for. Random casts may bring a fish or two, but it is difficult to determine closely the positions in which trout may be; and, even if it were always possible to determine their position, the size of the fish would not induce the angler to waste much effort upon them. A strong rift of fair depth, however, probably harbours as many trout and will prove as productive to the average angler as any half dozen selected pools.

The character of these rifts changes so frequently that it would be useless to attempt to describe where trout may be found in them when the water is high. Furthermore, a cast here and there is quite as likely to fall within sight of roving fish that are not averse to travelling some distance to take the fly as a cast placed with intent to cover a particular spot. The most likely place, however, is along the side of the centre of the heaviest current, the fly being so placed that it will travel at the same speed as the leader and line, or a trifle faster.

When the stream begins to fall, instinct warns the trout that he must take up less unstable quarters. He fixes upon a permanent home, and only moves therefrom when there is another rise in the stream or during his nocturnal roamings in search of food.

In early spring, when the stream is high, trout are roaming about and may be found almost anywhere. When such conditions prevail it is not uncommon to hear anglers say that most of their fish were taken on the rifts. There are times during this season when it is more than likely that the rifts will be the only stretches that prove fruitful. When such is the case the angler, while he should never overlook the pools, should spend most of his time on the swift water.

On one occasion, while fishing a stream which empties into the Delaware, near Narrowsburg, N. Y., I walked two miles down-stream to the stretch which I had chosen for my afternoon's sport. My first cast was made close to two o'clock, and at six o'clock I had taken over twenty fish, four of which, weighing over five and one half pounds, I killed, and twice as many more of the same size I returned to the stream. I got out of the stream at about the same spot I had entered it, having fished not over one hundred yards in four hours. The fish were taken in a broken rift; it seemed as if each rock in it was the hiding-place of a good one; and, though the current was quite swift, the floating fly was taken in each case slowly and deliberately. They were, it is true, not so large as one might have hoped to get in some of the deeper pools, but fair fish, nevertheless; and, as about half of them were rainbow trout, interest in the sport did not flag for a moment.

In a short rift or run forming the connecting-link between two pools, fish from both will be found occupying it when feeding, occasionally during the day, but usually at night, at which time minnows and other small fish may be picked up. Sometimes a good fish will remain in this water, but, because of the facility afforded him for entering it from above or below, this is not often the case. While this stretch is less fruitful than another which I will try to describe, it should never be carelessly fished; and, if the instructions given in this chapter for fishing the swift are followed, the effort should not go unrewarded. Many of these short rifts are met with in a day's fishing and too often are slighted by those careless anglers who seem anxious only to have their flies upon the surface of pools. They should be given careful attention, let conditions be what they may.

There are other rifts where the current seems to be travelling at its greatest speed and where the fall is sharp and continuous. Where the decline ends abruptly a pool is formed; where it is gradual, and the force of the current is spent, it spreads, fan-like, over the formation of gravel and stones, finally flowing to one bank or the other, forming another pool or another rift. The fish occupying these longer rifts or rapids may not be the largest in the stream, but are likely to be well above the average in size and worth trying for. Along both sides of the swiftest part of the current the fly may be floated successfully. A long line is inadvisable unless the angler has mastered the difficulty of handling it under such circumstances, because it is returned very quickly. He should pick out the "oily" looking spots upon which to place the fly, because there is less likelihood of its being drenched than if it is placed in the breaking water.

Conforming to the custom among many anglers, and for lack of a better term, I include in the term "rifts" those parts of the stream which, in my opinion, are the finest of all places to fish. I refer to the stretches where great boulders, and small ones too, protruding above the surface of the water, divide the current, which flows quietly but steadily between and around them.

In many cases it will be found that the banks on either side of such stretches, while not precipitous, are higher than where they border the wider parts of the stream. The bed being narrower, the depth of water will be found greater. For these reasons such sections are chosen by trout when the stream is low. The shady part of this water, if there be any, should be approached first, particularly if the weather be bright and the water low. Each boulder, in turn, should be carefully and thoroughly searched with the fly. The first attempt may be made between any two rocks, not too widely separated, at the bottom or down-stream end of the stretch, the fly being placed directly between and a foot above them. After several casts have been made the fly may be thrown a foot or two farther up-stream but in line with the previous casts.

Fishing the fly between such boulders serves a double purpose. As the fish lie alongside or just above them, the fly is readily seen from either position, and if it is taken near one of them the angler is saved the necessity of fishing the others, the indications being that the fish are ready to feed and that they may be lured away from their stands. On most occasions, however, the fish will be found just above the boulder and on the shady side, and the fly, persistently delivered in that position, will attract many of them.

The angler should remember that the backwater formed by the current flowing against the up-stream side of a boulder is a favourite haunt of brown trout, and should assume that the fish in the stretch occupy such positions until some indication is given that they do not. He should so present the fly that the fish is afforded a fair view of it and is not asked to come too far to take it. Rough water should be avoided when possible; but the fly should be floated on or near the swiftest part of the current, and this will usually be found close to the boulder.

When the boulders in a stretch are irregularly scattered, the course of the current being deflected by them so that the water twists and turns to escape the obstacles in its path, each one may harbour a good fish. Not one of them should escape the attention of the angler. Even those which appear to be in shallow water are worthy of consideration and sometimes yield large fish. The eddies behind them may be fished as much as he pleases, but he should not forget that on the up-stream side the greater number of fish will be found. He should avoid haste, and also the conclusion that because a fish is not risen in one spot there is none occupying it. If by carelessness, he drives out a fish, his chance of taking one higher up in the same stretch is jeopardised.

Where the current is direct in its flow, travelling, apparently, through what might be called a lane of boulders, the fish, if feeding, may be looked for in its middle along its entire course, as well as beside and above the rocks. Beginning at the bottom, the water for a very short distance may be covered from a point directly below; but after that the casts should be made at an angle of about forty-five degrees from either side, so that the fish, which may have been under the fly and have been unmoved by it, will not see the angler or his line. A sight of the line moves fish in a way that is very distressing to the angler responsible for it.

Of similar character are those stretches where the rapid current dashes against and around the boulders in them. From a distance one of these stretches appears to be a mass of tossing water, where the dry fly might be expected to be hopelessly out of place. In such parts of the stream the fall is quite sharp, the water tumbling over a succession of diminutive falls, presenting, when viewed from below, an appearance of great turbulence. Upon close inspection, however, there will be found between the boulders miniature pools, popularly called "pockets," where the current, while strong, is not direct, a great part of its force being spent in seeking new channels.

Beginning at the bottom row of the pockets, the tail of the lowest is cast over with as short a line as may be used consistently with precision. Where the water glides swiftly over the lip of the pocket the fly should be placed above and in such position that in its course down-stream it will pass close to the boulder which is deflecting the deeper and stronger part of the current. As the fly passes the boulder it should be lifted quickly but quietly from the water. A false cast or two should be made to dry it, and then it should be placed in exactly the same position as before, this procedure being continued until a rise is effected or the angler is prompted to abandon the spot. The fly may then be advanced a short distance at a time, the longitudinal position remaining the same, until the water in a straight line up-stream between the boulder and the head of the pocket is covered. The other side should then be fished in the same manner, and this without the angler having changed his own position, which should have been assumed at the start with reference to the availability of all parts of the water.

Each pocket will present practically the same features. The depth may be greater in one, the current stronger in another, but the boulders at the head and tail should be the objective points for the angler's fly in every case. Where the depth is great or the current strong, more persistence upon the part of the angler is demanded—compensated, as a rule, by a larger fish. Where the water, with but a gentle wrinkle, slips by the boulder and does not break into a fall, the fly should be placed a yard above and directly in front of the boulder, and should not be retrieved until it has passed some distance down-stream. A fish in the dead water may often be tempted to come down after the fly, and when this happens the whole scene is enacted in plain view. There is nothing quite so exciting as this in the whole sport of angling except, perhaps, casting to and inducing a fish to rise that is lying in plain view.

Trout frequently take up stations in the backwater or eddy which is formed under and behind the miniature falls in these rapid stretches. When in this position they are inaccessible to the dry fly angler. They belong entirely to the wet fly man who is familiar enough with the habits of the fish to drop his fly above the brink of the fall, allowing it to be carried over and then under the water, so that, if it is caught in the backwater, it is presented directly to the fish, which rarely refuses to take one that comes so easily. When evening comes on, however, the dry fly angler has his opportunity. The sizable fish which select these retreats during the bright days drop down-stream as darkness approaches, and, if not cruising, will be found just where the current spends itself, or under and below the little eddies to the side. These eddies should be scrutinized closely if insects are upon the water. The presence of the fish will be indicated by the rise to the flies which collect there. Should there be no insects about, the fish may be induced to rise by casting repeatedly in the quieting water.

Perhaps no water on our American streams appeals more to the average angler than a beautiful pool; and yet rarely does this water fulfil the promise it seems to hold out. That pools do contain trout, and sometimes very large ones, is true; but the fact that the fish may remain unmoved, after every artifice of the angler has been exhausted in an attempt to induce them to rise, is very discouraging. This not unusual experience may be the foundation for the belief many anglers have that the larger fish have ceased to be surface feeders and cannot be persuaded to rise to a small insect. To get one of these big fish with the floating fly the angler must have "luck"—that luck which brings him upon the stream when the fish are near the surface. Success on waters of this kind depends quite as much upon the mood of the fish as upon the skill of the angler.

If the fish are feeding, or are ready to feed, upon winged insects, they will be found in a position from which the angler's fly may be seen, in which event he may hope to bring them to the artificial. But no amount of skill will induce a rise if the fish are hidden in the strongholds with which these rocky pools abound. It is absurd to expect that a big fish, lying near the bottom of a pool which may have six or eight feet of water in it, will come that distance upon the first appearance of a tiny morsel of food upon the surface. A fish that has retired to deep water is not interested in food; or, if he is, only caddis larvæ, dobsons, etc., that may be picked up on the bottom, or some other sort of food considerably under the surface, will attract his attention.

Trout fortunate enough to escape the many dangers which beset them in our streams grow to great size and become largely nocturnal feeders. Night feeding is an instinct of the fish, though the smaller ones are forced by the appetite of youth to seek food in daylight, also. This is why a pool that looks as if it should contain a big fish (and probably does) yields but a few dandiprats when the condition of the water has been unchanged for any length of time. The big fish are not ravenous enough to be seeking food all of the time, and the little chaps have undisputed possession of the open water. A wonderful change in the mood of these large fish takes place when the stream is freshened after a fall of rain. The artificial fly is then taken in the most deliberate and certain manner—taken by the fish as if they knew it as a member of a family with which they have been acquainted all their lives, although it may not bear the slightest resemblance to any living insect. At such times the angler is apt to lose faith in the much-vaunted wariness and cunning of the fish and may foolishly ascribe his remarkable success to his own skill. Whether the change of water invigorates trout, or instinct tells them that they may expect food to be washed down to them, it is certain that the desire to feed is aroused, and they are at these times neither fastidious nor discriminating.

Several years ago on a stream in Sullivan County, the name of which I have promised to forget, I was in the brook just after the top of a flood and found the fish so willing that, for the particular day, at any rate, I was ready to believe the story told of some northern waters where the fish "were so numerous and so hungry that one had to hide behind a tree to bait the hook." Nearly every cast brought a slow, deliberate, businesslike rise—all large fish for so small a stream. I killed two fish that weighed one pound five ounces, and one pound nine ounces, respectively. One of these fish had two crawfish in its stomach, freshly taken; the other had a small stone catfish, pretty well digested;

there was nothing else in either—not an insect of any sort. The next day was practically a repetition of the previous one—two fish killed, both just over one pound five ounces. The stomach and gullet of one were absolutely empty; the other contained a single June-bug, freshly taken, and, among a number of other insects, a waterstrider, long thought by anglers to form no part of the trout's menu. I have never been able to quite satisfy myself that this particular experience was of any great value except that it strengthened my belief that trout are moved to feed by changes in the stream caused by flood waters running down. Perhaps, also, it tended to prove that there were more big fish in the stream than I would have believed without the experience. All my fish were taken at the lips of the pools which abound in this rock-bedded stream, and I devoted my time exclusively to those places, in the hope of securing a really good fish. No small fish rose to the fly, although they are a-plenty in the stream. They had evidently been driven to other water by fear of their older brothers.

The greatest essential to success in fly fishing, wet or dry, is stream knowledge; by which I mean, not necessarily familiarity with the stream actually being fished, but that general knowledge, based on careful study of the habits of the fish, that enables the angler to select the proper part of the current in which to place the fly. Such selection is of the greatest importance when pools are being fished— it is next in importance to keeping out of sight of the trout. Under no circumstances should a pool be approached with the idea of placing the first cast in what appears to be the likeliest spot, as there is always danger of frightening the fish off if he should happen to be somewhere else in the pool. Before a fly is placed on the water, a careful study should be made of its depths and currents. If the large fish are surface feeding, they may be looked for in two places particularly: it the very lip of the pool or in the eddies at the head.

The indication that a fish is feeding at the lip or bottom of a pool is unmistakable. While the actual taking of the insect may be accomplished quietly, the fish lies sometimes so close to the surface where the water spills out that the sharp recovery necessary in the quickening water reveals his position. This is a difficult fish to take, for the reason that, lying as he does in the shallower water—which, as a rule, has a smooth surface—he is very apt to see the angler. A long line must be used, which adds to the difficulty, as it is almost impossible to keep the line out of the swift water below the lip which snatches the fly away from the fish before he has even had a good look at it. A proper presentation may be made, however, and this annoying drag avoided, if the cast is so delivered that the line falls upon one of the stones or boulders which form the lip of the pool. The fly will then float naturally, without being pulled, until it reaches the point where the water spills out, which point it must be allowed to pass before being retrieved. If no rise is effected the cast may be repeated, and continued as long as the fish is still in position. No connection need be looked for, however, unless the fly is placed fairly close to and above the fish, and marked acceleration of pace avoided. Where there are no kindly boulders to help the angler in his deception, a chance—though a remote one—may be taken by presenting the fly in the hope that it may be taken at once, because of its accurate delivery, and before there is any drag upon it.

If, at the moment of the angler's arrival at a pool, there are no insects upon the water there will be no rise to indicate the position of a fish. But it does not follow that one is not in position and ready to feed. In this case even greater care should be exercised in approaching the lip of the pool than if a rise had been actually observed. If the angler does his work well, and has a sharp eye, the fish may often be seen lying along the side of the current as the water spills out, or just above some small boulder or other obstruction to the water's course. Sometimes the boulders may be completely under water, but their presence is denoted by a wrinkling of the surface, and the fish may be looked for just above them.

The angler must work out the problem of properly presenting the fly at each pool. In no case, however, where the fish is seen or his position is indicated by his activities should the fly be cast directly over him. It should always be cast to one side or the other, slightly above, and at an angle. This suggestion may be safely followed in every case where fish are seen and it is possible to so cast from the position occupied by the angler. When the fish are found to be occupying positions at the tail of pools—whether it be early morning, or just at dusk, or, as it sometimes happens, at midday—they are almost invariably ready to feed; and, while not always interested in insects, they are frequently induced to take the artificial because it appears close to them. Though there may have been no indication that the large fish have dropped back from the deeper water to the lip of the pool, the angler's actions should always be governed by the assumption that they are in that position until he is convinced that they are not. If he has been incautious the widening wake marking the fish's swift dart up-stream makes it quite certain that the hope of taking a trout from that particular pool must be deferred. Small fish occupying this "tail position" are as easily frightened off by sight of the angler as the large ones are, and their alarm, being communicated to the fish above, destroys whatever chance there might otherwise have been on the upper water. It is the carelessness with which the average angler overlooks this important part of the pool that is responsible for the many failures registered on what should be productive water.

It frequently happens, particularly when the water is low and bright and has not been recently disturbed, that trout are lying a few yards above the lip of the pool in the quiet water. The presence of the fish is disclosed by the wake made by him in his rush for a fly that has been presented somewhere near him. The direction the fish is taking is easily discernible, and, if he is headed down-stream —which is often the case—the situation is one that requires the gentlest possible handling. The angler should remain motionless, leaving his fly upon the water even at the risk of having the line become entangled about his feet, because the fish, being headed in the angler's direction, will be quick to detect any motion; and the rod should not be moved under any consideration. The fish, after having composed himself, will be headed up-stream again and, if not actually seen by the angler, may be assumed to be where the wake ended.

It is quite usual for a fish, after having made a rush toward the fly, to abandon the chase when the fly approaches too closely to the spill, to assume a position where he stopped, and to wait there for another insect to come down. This is the angler's opportunity; but if it is to be of any advantage to him deliberation must mark his every action. The fly must be dropped gently over the marked spot and should not be retrieved until it has passed below the rod. It will be difficult to overcome the impulse to retrieve the fly, even though it is getting farther beyond control all the time; but, as the fish has possibly been interested in it and, having turned, will immediately detect any action of the rod and be off at once, such impulse must be resisted. By stripping the line in with the disengaged hand, the fly may be recovered and presented again. Until the fly is taken by the fish, or until the angler is convinced that it will not be taken, every motion should be very deliberate. If the fish is not risen on the first cast, each succeeding throw should be made a little farther upstream than the previous one, until the point where the fish was first seen is reached. The fly should not be retrieved in any case until it has passed over the water covered before—and it should travel in the same lane after each cast. A fish spotted as described will surely fall to the rod if the angler is careful, and his taking will afford some of the most pleasurable moments spent upon the stream.

When the angler decides to abandon the lower end of

the pool, it is much wiser for him to use a longer line to reach the upper water than it is to advance up-stream, because by wading up he may frighten a fish lying in the part of the pool already covered and thus warn off the ones above. The entire pool should be carefully scanned for indications of feeding fish before any attempt is made to cast over the upper part of it. The eddies on either side of the main current at the head of the pool should be given particular attention. Should a large fish inhabit the pool the eddy will be his dining-room. He will occupy it, however, only at certain intervals, and, if the angler should be fortunate enough to arrive at a time when he is seeking food, it ought to yield a fine trout. Rarely meeting competition, because of their size, the fish in these eddies are very deliberate in their feeding—securing such insects as may be on the surface with but little effort. For this reason many opportunities are missed by the unobservant angler who fails to notice the gentle wrinkling of the surface, or the small bubble left upon it, as the fish sucks in some tiny insect, and by the careless angler who sees the slight disturbance, and attributes it to a small fish. Some of the largest fish I have ever killed gave no indication of their size as the fly was taken, and not until they had fastened did I realise how heavy they were. The slightest indication of action in the eddy should be investigated thoroughly with the fly; for, while only a small fish may be taken in one, the next may produce "the big fish."

Throwing to a fish in the eddy of a pool requires some care, but a close study of the currents will make it comparatively easy. Trout always lie with heads to the current, and those in an eddy are no exception; consequently, they will be headed *down-stream,* or against the current, which is flowing *up.* This position of the fish must be taken into consideration when the fly is to be presented from below, and the angler will find that his greatest difficulty will be in keeping out of sight. How he may do this he must decide for himself, but, even at the risk of being seen, he should cast up-stream from *directly below* the fish; *i.e.,* from a position on the same side of the swift current as the eddy he is fishing. If the fly is dropped in that part of the current which is turning up-stream it will be carried to the fish in a natural manner, and if care has been taken in placing the line loosely in the comparatively dead water below, the progress of the fly will not be impeded. If the fish has been well spotted, the fly should be dropped a foot or two below him, and always in that current which will bring it directly to him. In this particular situation the first cast should be the telling one, because if the fly is not taken it is not returned to the angler immediately, and its retrieve against the current is likely to be disturbing to the fish. If the fly has been carried over and beyond the spot where the rise was seen, it does not follow that it has passed over the fish and been refused. He may be backing up under it, and may take it a yard from where he is presumed to be, if it travel that far. However, if satisfied that the fly is not going to appeal to the fish—which conclusion should not be reached until the fly is no longer in a natural position—the retrieve may be made very slowly and carefully, after which the angler may wait a minute or two, or until the fish rises again.

Sometimes the fly will be carried by the eddy toward the swift, down-stream current and be caught in it. In this event, it is easily retrieved without disturbing the water in the vicinity of the fish, and may be presented again immediately. A fish should not be given up while continuing to rise steadily; he will become accustomed to the artificial, and will take it in time, if its action is not unnatural. An eddy should be fished in the same careful manner whether a fish is seen feeding in it or not; but, in the latter case, while a fish may be in position and ready to feed, the varying currents and the difficulty encountered in attempting to retrieve the fly delicately against them destroy its natural action, and prevent, to a certain extent, proper simulation of a "hatch." The fly can cover but a short distance before it is necessary to retrieve it, and this makes for rather tedious work, because it must be brought back slowly and gently until it is out of the eddy before it is taken from the water. In this connection, it may be borne in mind that it is possible to decoy a fish from the eddy by placing the fly on the edge of the swift, down-stream current nearest the eddy, permitting it to float down three or four yards each time. If a half dozen casts have brought no response, it is better to discontinue casting than to risk driving the fish to another part of the pool, and thus disturb some other fish that might have fallen to the rod later had it remained unmolested.

CHAPTER V

THE IMITATION OF THE NATURAL INSECT

ITHIN a very recent period it has been asserted, upon scientific authority, that fish are colour-blind. If this be true, though it is diffiicult for the mere angler to understand how it may be proven, the theory of those who believe that it is necessary to imitate in the artificial fly the colour of the insects upon which trout feed must be abandoned.

Writing upon the subject no longer ago than 1904, Sir Herbert Maxwell, certainly a competent observer, said: "My own experience goes to convince me that salmon, and even highly educated chalk-stream trout, are singularly indifferent to the colours of flies offered to them, taking a scarlet or blue fly as readily as one closely assimilated to the natural insect. Probably the position of the floating lure, between the fish's eye and the light, interferes with any nice discrimination of hue from reflected rays."

Cotton and the many angling writers who followed him all dwelt with insistence upon the necessity for close imitation, especially in relation to colour. In 1740 John Williamson stated the principle in the following words: ". . . as the great Difficulty is to obtain the Colour of the *Fly* which the Fish take at the Instant of your Angling, it is impos-

97

sible to give any certain Directions on that Head; because several Rivers and Soils are haunted by peculiar Sorts of Flies, and the Flies that come usually in such a Month of the Year, may the succeeding Year come almost a Month sooner or later as the Season proves colder or hotter. Tho' some Fish change their Fly once or twice in one Day, yet usually they seek not for another Sort, till they have for some Days glutted themselves with a former, which is commonly when those Flies are near Death, or ready to go out." Then, giving some simple instructions in regard to tying flies, he quotes Walton: "But to see a Fly made by an Artist is the best Instruction; after which the Angler may walk by the River, and mark what Flies fall on the Water that Day, and catch one of them, if he see the *Trouts* leap at a Fly of that Kind. . . ." Williamson's book was practically a compilation, containing the best of what had been written by anglers before him, together with his own observations.

From Williamson's time no work on fly fishing seemed complete unless instructions were given in the art of fly making, with a description of the sorts and colours of furs, silks, feathers, etc., suitable for the imitation of the natural insects held to be so necessary; but until the appearance in 1836 of Ronalds's "Fly Fishers' Entomology," it cannot be said of any author that the instructions given by him were the result of scientific study. Ronalds was most thorough in his investigation, and his experiments in regard to the senses of taste and hearing of trout are extremely interesting and instructive. While his conclusions run counter to the opinions of many other angling writers, to my mind they appear logical and are convincing; and I think he proves that trout do not have the senses of taste and hearing developed to the degree of acuteness attributed to them by other writers. Following some advice as to the choice of flies, Ronalds says: "It should never be forgotten that, let the state of weather or the water be what it may, success in fly fishing very much depends upon showing the fish a good imitation, both in colour and size, of that insect which he has recently taken; an exact resemblance of the *shape* does not seem to be quite as essential a requisite as that of colour, since the former varies according to the position of the insect either in or upon the water; but a small fly is usually employed when the water is fine, because the fish is then better enabled to detect an imitation and because the small fly is more easily imitated. The resemblance of each particular colour, etc., is not required to be so exact as in the case of a large fly." Notwithstanding his evident preference for colour over shape or form, Ronalds was careful to have the proportions of his imitations exact. The many editions of his work that have been issued, and the frequent reference made to him by later writers, is evidence that his opinions are held in high regard by anglers.

About three years before the "Fly Fishers' Entomology" appeared, Professor James Rennie, in his "Alphabet of Scientific Angling," ridiculed the theory of imitation. He says: "It is still more common, however, for anglers to use artificial baits, made in imitation or pretended imitation, of those that are natural. I have used the phrase 'pretended imitation' as strictly applicable to by far the greater number of what are called by anglers artificial flies, because these rarely indeed bear the most distant resemblance to any living fly or insect whatever, though, if exact imitation were an object, there can be little doubt that it could be accomplished much more perfectly than is ever done in any of the numerous artificial flies made by the best artists in that line of work. The fish, indeed, appear to seize an artificial fly because, when drawn by the angler along the water, it has the appearance of being a living insect, whose species is quite unimportant, as all insects are equally welcome, though the larger they are, as in the case of grasshoppers, so much the better, because they then furnish a better mouthful. The aim of the angler, accordingly, ought to be to have his artificial fly calculated, by its form and colours, to attract the notice of the fish, in which case he has a much greater chance of success than by making the greatest efforts to imitate any particular species of fly." That this statement caused considerable discussion—probably because it was made by a professor of zoology—is evidenced by the appearance in 1838 of "A True Treatise of the Art of Fly-Fishing," written by those strong advocates of the imitation theory, William Shipley and Edward Fitzgibbon, who devoted a whole chapter to controverting the professor's theories, calling upon the writings of Bainbridge, Best, Taylor, Davy, Ronalds, and others in support of their opinions, concluding with the statement that "they flattered themselves that they had triumphantly done so." It seems to me that, though they argued with vigour and vehemence, they have proven nothing, conclusively, except their ability to place a construction upon the professor's statements that afforded them an opportunity for the discussion. A careful reading of Rennie shows that he merely expressed the opinion that the greatest efforts of the angler should be to make his fly one that would attract the notice of the fish by its form and colour, rather than to imitate any particular species of fly. To be sure, we have no knowledge of what his ideas with regard to form and colour were; we may assume, however, that he believed that if a red fly four inches long with yellow and blue wings and a green tail would attract the fish, such would be the fly to use. The illustration is absurd, of course; but we have a right to infer that his belief was that any form or colour which would attract the fish would do. He advanced the theory that the trout took the artificial because they were near-sighted; apparently he did not believe that they took it because they were colour-blind.

The English creation known as the "Alexandra," representing absolutely nothing in insect life (at least to eye of man), strongly supports Professor Rennie's theory. Its effect upon trout has been so deadly that it has been suggested by many English anglers that its use should be barred upon some streams. In the same class with the Alexandra might be placed our own American nondescript, the "Parmacheene Belle," the invention of Mr. Henry P. Wells, whose theory was, "An imitation of some favourite food is in itself sufficient under all circumstances, provided it is so conspicuous as readily to be seen . . . and the fly in question was made, imitating the colour of the belly fin of the trout itself." This theory may be sound enough, but in this particular application of it one is asked to believe that the trout is inordinately fond of the belly fin of its relatives, which seems to me to be straining credulity overfar. To some old cannibalistic fish these fins may be attractive. I do not deny it, for I do not know; but in my own experience I have not known them to be plucked or bitten from the victim; nor are they found floating about loose. The Parmacheene Belle is undoubtedly an imitation of the belly fin of a trout, but it is not an imitation of any favourite food of the fish. Its value as a lure is well known to those who fish in the lakes and streams of Canada and Maine, but trout do not take it because they recognise it as a familiar article of diet. They probably take it because of its brilliant colour, in which respect it embodies Professor Rennie's idea of what a "fly" should be. Being made up of reds and whites, it probably reflects more light than do sombre-hued patterns and, consequently, is the more easily seen. As a rule, it is taken under water, and most often after it has sunk to considerable depth.

Speaking of the Alexandra, Mr. Halford says: "It certainly is not the imitation of any indigenous insect known to entomologists; possibly the bright silver body moving through the river gives some idea of the gleam of a minnow. Long ere this its use should have been prohibited on every stream frequented by the *bona-fide* fly-fisherman, as it is a dreadful scourge to any water, scratching and frightening an immense proportion of the trout which are tempted to follow it." If this means anything, it means that trout are at first attracted by the fly or lure, but upon closer inspection discover the cheat, and, taking it uncertainly, are often slightly pricked, or, refusing it entirely, are sometimes scraped by the hook as they turn away. This criticism, it seems to me, might be directed equally well against any creation of feathers, fur, and tinsel that is fished sunk.

While rather off the main point, I may be so bold as to say that, while the sunk fly method does not appeal to me at all, I cannot readily see that it scratches many fish or frightens them in any way; and, if it did, the recollection of the affair would not linger long enough in the trout's memory to injure the chances of his being taken the next day on a dry fly, or even on another sunk one. Mr. G. E. M. Skues, who advocates the use of the sunk fly on the same streams where correct imitations are presented to rising fish, says that he presents imitations of the nymphæ in the positions occupied by the naturals; that he rarely scratches a fish, and hooks but very few foul. The inference in this case might be that the trout fastens to an imitation more readily than to an Alexandra—one really deluding the fish by its natural appearance, the other exciting only its curiosity or ire.

While exhibiting an admirable filial loyalty, many of us have been prone to be governed by tradition, and the education we received in the beginning from our fathers. With few exceptions, we have trudged along the beaten path, looking rarely to right or left, but backward a great deal, using the same flies our fathers used before us, emulating their methods, and admiring their successes. We have overlooked the fact that we are contending with conditions that have decreased the number of native trout, and that would have taxed even the great skill with which we have endowed those of loving memory. I remember that one of my father's favourite flies was the Queen-of-the Waters. Naturally it became one of mine, and I used it religiously—remembering its successes, forgetting its failures. A story connected with this fly may prove interesting, and perhaps tend to show how close I was to becoming a confirmed colourist, or, rather, a strong believer in the trout's ability to detect colour.

Many years ago, while preparing for a short trip to the stream, I discovered that I did not have a single Queen-of-the-Waters in my fly book. On my way to the railroad station I stopped in a tackle shop and asked for a dozen of that pattern. The clerk was unable to find any in stock, but suggested that I try a dozen called King-of-the Waters. Although there was, in fact, little similarity between these two patterns except in the name itself, this seemed sufficient to my ignorant mind, and I took them. The following day, upon the stream, my cast of three flies (I was a wet fly angler then) was never without a King-of-the-Waters —and not a fish did I take with it. I attributed my nonsuccess to the pattern of fly, and it never occurred to me at the time that very few fish were taken at all that day, although many anglers were on the stream. The next morning, when I opened my fly book, I found that a great deal of the red dye used upon the silk body of the fly had come off on the drying pad. The body of the fly was now a beautiful pink. Out of curiosity I wet the fly, and the pink body turned a brilliant red. I thought the thing over, and decided that I had stumbled upon an explanation of the failure of the fly to take the day before. The body of the fly originally was red and was evidently meant to appear so to the trout. When wet, however, it had turned a muddy brown. With most of the colour washed out, the fly turned a darker shade when wet, became really red, and stayed red. I determined that if this was the colour the trout wanted, they should have it, and I soaked a half dozen flies in a tumbler of water, pressing and squeezing every bit of dyestuff out of them that I could. They were all pink-bodied when I had finished with them. Recollections of the following day are still fresh in my mind. The fish seemed frantic to get my fly. I used one as the stretcher, and it was taken almost to the utter exclusion of the other patterns above. I remember that, while sitting upon a boulder in midstream tying another pink fly on in place of the hand dropper, as an experiment, I lost it in the swift current, and felt almost as badly as if I had lost a friend. The fly used as a dropper was taken readily, but not so often as when used as a stretcher, yet often enough to make me feel that I had made a great discovery. Since then, however, I have often wondered if it really were a discovery, or if, indeed, the old Queen-of-the-Waters, under the circumstances and conditions prevailing at the time, would not have been just as killing, and probably just as great a failure the preceding day.

Many years have passed, and I am still using the pink-bodied fly, modified in form, however, but never the Queen-of-the-Waters. I cannot say that I think it takes any better than the Whirling Dun or the Pale Evening Dun, which are among my favourites. Frequently, when I have

found the pink-bodied fly taking well, I have changed
immediately to one of the others, and have found no
marked difference in their taking qualities. The pink-
bodied fly in its present form—that is, tied in accordance
with my own practice—has upright wings and a tail, and
in appearance is not unlike the Red Spinner. It has been
dubbed the "Pink Lady" by one of my friends, a name that
it seems destined to carry, as it has already appeared by
that name in a tackle dealer's catalogue. As to whether or
not the trout is attracted by the brilliancy of the body, or
by the rib of gold tinsel that gives it a fillip other flies lack,
or because it bears a fairly close resemblance to the Red
Spinner, I cannot venture an opinion. That it is a taking
fly, however, I have demonstrated many times upon the
stream. I am inclined to believe that its typical form,
rather than its colour, appeals to the fish. Opposed to my
opinion, however, is that of many of my friends who use
it, one of them, in particular, contending that the pink-
bodied fly will take fish anywhere at any time. He firmly
believes that its colour constitutes its charm. It is an interesting fact, considered in this connection, that the gentleman himself is, to some extent, colour-blind.

Objects floating upon the surface of a shallow stream
reflect the colour of the bottom in varying degree, according to their density. A number of white objects floating
above a moss or grass covered bottom reflect different tones
of green, that one which is most opaque showing the dark-
est shade, and each one reflecting a lighter tone in proportion to the amount of light that filters through it. It is true,
of course, that a yellow insect floating over this same

bottom would reflect a shade of green all its own, and it is but natural to assume that if the same shade or tint of yellow is used in the artificial, its employment would more nearly approximate the effect of reflection upon the natural insect; but if the exact shade or tint is important, the effect is not produced unless the same amount of light passes through both natural and artificial. The use of the hook itself precludes the possibility of any delicate imitation of nature, and the infinite pains anglers have taken to make representations of the segmentations of many of the *Ephemeridæ* by using quill windings for the body would seem to be for naught, except in so far as they affect the artistic eye of those using them. Many such flies undoubtedly take fish, but I dare say not because they represent particularly the *colour* of the natural.

It would seem, therefore, that the most important consideration of the fly-tier who seeks to imitate the colour of the natural insect should be the materials to be used. Consequently he should select only those which are transparent, or at least translucent, and that reflect the surroundings as readily as the natural insect does as it floats down-stream on the surface of the water. It is, of course, quite obvious that the artificial, no matter how cleverly it may be fashioned, cannot present the same appearance of translucence as the natural; but one skilfully made of the appropriate materials will approximate it nearly enough for all practical purposes. I believe that the effect produced by reflection of the colour of the bottom is not so marked upon an insect resting with its legs upon the surface and its body above it, as it is upon the insect with its body directly on the surface. If the artificial could always be cast so that it rested only upon its hackle, perhaps the difference between it and the natural would not be so marked. This may be accomplished, perhaps, by those anglers who are wedded to fishing the rise, and who keep their fly absolutely dry until a fish is seen feeding, but it is asking too much of those who enjoy seeing their fly upon the water over likely places.

Although, in certain species of insects which interest anglers, the difference in size and colour between the sexes is not great, in others it is quite marked; and some anglers are of the opinion that an imitation of the female of a species is a more killing pattern than one of the male. A most ingenious explanation of the fish's preference for the female insect was offered by the Reverend J. G. Wood in his "Insects at Home," published in 1871. He says: "Should the reader be an angler, he will recognise in the female pseudimago the 'Green Drake,' and in the perfect insect the 'Grey Drake.' The angler only cares for the female insects, because the fish prefer them, laden as they are with eggs, to the males, which have little in them but air." The statement certainly endows the trout with a fine sense of discrimination and taste. That the female insects are preferred by the trout may possibly be true, but it is to be regretted that the author did not explain how he arrived at the conclusion that they are preferred because they carry eggs. If he was an angler himself, it was probably the result of personal experience in the use of either the insect or its imitation; or autopsies upon fish may have revealed the fact. In the latter case, the discovery of a preponderating

number of females in the stomach of the fish would naturally influence his opinion; but even this discovery could
hardly be said to prove that the trout had a preference
for the female because it was "laden with eggs." If our
auther did not fish for trout, his knowledge may have been
based either upon information obtained from some angler
or upon his own observation of feeding fish; in the latter
case, being more of an entomologist than an angler, it is
not unreasonable to suppose that his interest was centred
upon the insect, and not upon the fish. Having seen a number of females taken in succession—probably at a time
when they were predominant—the fact would indicate to
his scientific mind a preference for the sex on the part of
the fish.

If the fish does in fact prefer the female, the explanation
may be found in the life history of the May-fly, which indicates that the male, some time after the sexual function
is performed, falls lifeless, while the female, shortly after
intercourse, hovers over the water, and, touching the surface with that part of her body carrying the now fertile
eggs, deposits them as nature has decreed. It is this action,
made in a succession of dips, the insect finally resting upon
the water, which presents that appearance of life so attractive to feeding fish, trout naturally ignoring a dead insect
when their attention is attracted to a fluttering one. If trout
never took the male insect, nothing would be gained by
imitating it; but they do—though when they do, it is generally because there are no interfering females about; or, to
be more gallant, when the more attractive sex is not
strongly in evidence. It naturally suggests itself to the

angler that when the females of any species are predominant upon the water, it is advantageous to present a close
imitation of them in colour and size—the form of the sexes
being similar.

It seems to me that the colourist, as a rule, is much too
certain that his flies appear to the trout as they do to his
own sense of sight; surely, there is no way of demonstrating or establishing what the truth may be. Certain it is that
up to the present time, it has not been possible to fashion an
artificial fly that would give even a faint semblance of the
translucence of the natural insect; and this, it seems to
me, is a very important consideration. Using materials
available, it is quite impossible to duplicate this delicate
appearance of the live insect, and my own conclusion is
that materials which will most nearly represent it by permitting a filtering of light are the ones to be employed—
preferably materials of quiet tone and colour.

I am of the opinion, also, that the colour, or perhaps the
transparency, of the wings of the artificial fly is quite as
important as the colour of the body; and I am satisfied, so
far as my own angling is concerned, that all erect-winged
flies should be tied with wings made of feathers from the
starling's wing, or flues from the inside wing feather of the
mallard or black duck. For, while trout may not be able
to distinguish quite so readily the colour of the wings out
of the water as the body of the fly on the water, the natural
appearance of the wings may prevent them from scrutinising the body too closely, and thus discovering discrepan-
cies in its coloring; and, while wings of light silvery grey
may not appear so to the fish, to my eye they produce a

close resemblance to the transparent, gauzy wing common to all of the *Ephemeridæ*, in both the dun and perfect states.

I have a decided preference for winged flies, but that is because they look more like living insects to me when they are on the water than do hackled flies, and not because I think they appear more natural or lifelike to the fish. In practice I have found that hackled flies are taken quite as readily floating as ever they were when I fished them under water, and it may very well be that the hackle fibres standing out from and around the body on and above the surface of the water are even a better imitation of the wings of the *Ephemeridæ* than are the feathers of the winged variety. Certainly a greater amount of light passes through them, and the result may be a better representation of the transparency and neuration of the wings of the natural insect than can he had from the use of artificial wings. At any rate, hackled flies float admirably, and the fish take them freely. And, although the dry fly anglers who use them may feel that something of form and appearance has been sacrificed to utility, their æsthetic sense will probably survive the shock when they find themselves successful—even those who insist that their fly be always beautifully cocked. If it is a consideration to be reckoned with, a hackled fly will outlast a dozen winged ones, being easily dried and humoured back into shape; while, on the other hand, a winged fly is almost hopelessly ruined when taken by a fish. In my own fishing I use a new fly over each fish—an extravagant habit, perhaps—but I love to see a natural looking artificial floating on the water. An old, mussed-up fly may continue to take fish as did the one fly we all have recollections of, that took fish until it was worn to ravelling, and no other would do; nevertheless, the use of a fresh fly is good insurance against defeat, and, aside from its extravagance, the practice is recommended.

If the angler is to fish with a floating fly, the necessity of some imitation of colour and form is quite evident, but imitation need not be carried to the extent of copying minute variation of colour in slavish detail. To copy the form of the natural fly is, of course, practically impossible. The quantity of hackle used on the artificial to represent the legs of the natural (which number six at most) could hardly be lessened, so great is its aid in floating the fly. Mr. Halford recommends tying the tail of the artificial in four whisks so as to increase its buoyancy, even though the setæ of the natural number but two in most cases—never more than three. The use of these parts in slightly exaggerated form does not denote a contempt for the keenness of the fish's vision on the part of the angler employing them. Rather, they are a necessary evil, and after all, show a divergence in form in no way so marked as that occasioned by the hook.

If approximately exact imitation of form of the dun or subimago of the *Ephemeridæ* is attempted, the wings of the artificial should be tied so as to stand close together and directly upright over the body. But a deviation from this form to the extent of having the wings separated will enable the angler to present the fly cocked more frequently, to drop it lightly, and will work but little harm.

In my own fishing I am willing to risk any defeat which

a slight variance in colour may invite, if the fly will float erect and in the place I wish it to. While delicacy in handling the line will place the fly upright more often than not, "cocking" of the fly is unfortunately not under direct control of the angler. "Cocking" is a very important part of the imitation of the natural insect—that imitation described as "position"—but it is not so essential as the accurate and delicate placing of the fly, which last depends entirely upon the skill of the angler. Perhaps "position" is best described by saying that it includes both "attitude" and "plane."

The plane in which the fly is to travel must be selected by the angler, and a combination of the judgment which prompts this selection, and the skill which maintains the plane during a great number of casts, will contribute more to success than the presentation of any particular pattern of fly. As a matter of fact, it is perhaps the only form of imitation which approximates nature—a fly sitting upon the water, being carried down-stream in the same current, and as unhampered and unrestrained in its action as a natural insect. Reliance upon certain patterns purporting to represent certain insects is never so strong again with the angler who, by his own skill, produces an imitation in this way that deludes a good fish. The governing consideration in the practice of this theory of imitation is the selection of the proper current in which to place the fly, and the angler, being guided naturally by his knowledge of the habits of the fish, should make a close study of the trend of the stream currents—particularly of those upon its surface—before beginning operations. Whether or not the fly is to be placed an inch from the bank, or a foot or two away, should depend entirely upon this observation, plane being always the important consideration.

The surface currents carry down numbers of insects, both dead and alive, and the edge of that one which is carrying most drift and is travelling slowest should be chosen by the angler for the delivery of the artificial— always with regard to the avoidance of drag. If there are no insects about or upon the surface of the water, small drift stuff, leaves, twigs, and the like will be carried down in the same plane, and under this surfaced drift the fish will probably be lying. He is interested in things upon the surface, and it is the angler's business to know it, and to so present the fly that it will come down as naturally as an unhampered insect.

It seems hardly necessary to state that it will be found well-nigh if not quite impossible to imitate the fluttering of a fly over or upon the water, by means of the rod. Yet many of us, when wet fly fishing, have deluded ourselves into the belief that, by the use of a dropper-fly and its careful manipulation, we were simulating, to a certain degree, the fluttering of the natural insect. At any rate, when the fly was taken we flattered ourselves that this was the case. Yet frequently, with the angler's attention centred upon giving to the dropper-fly a proper motion, the sub-merged tail-fly was taken, and usually by the larger fish. Instead of weakening one's faith in the dropper-fly and the efficacy of its jerky motion, experiences such as these have been known to strengthen a belief in the method; and I have heard the idea expressed that the action of the dropper-fly on the surface had attracted the attention of the fish to the tail-fly. This may be true, but as a matter of fact, the sunk fly was the better imitation of life, which perhaps accounts for the fish's preference for it.

Those who practised fly fishing in the manner described paid little regard to imitation of colour, and perhaps less to imitation of form; a comparison of the ordinary tackle-shop wet fly with the natural insect will convince any doubting angler that this is so. When they did attempt to imitate the colour of the natural fly, they were accustomed to give little or no thought to colour changes likely to take place upon immersion, with the result that in many cases where silk was used upon the body of the fly, these changes were great enough to destroy almost at once any resemblance to nature the artificial might have had before it was wet. I sometimes find myself believing that these anglers, when they considered colour at all, considered it only in relation to its effect upon their own eyes, and without any regard to the fish's view of it—perhaps not entirely without reason. True, the changes in, or loss of, colour were offset to a considerable extent by the motion, more or less rapid, imparted to the fly, which prevented close scrutiny by the trout, and detection of the fraud. My own notion is that as the fly had to be taken quickly by the fish, if at all, it was taken because it was moving and might be food of some sort and not because it looked like or was an imitation of any particular insect.

There are a great many expert anglers in America who fish with accurate or close imitations of the natural insect, wet or sunk, and who, by virtue of their skill in throwing the fly and their knowledge of the haunts and habits of the trout, are enabled to basket fish of fine quality and size —fish that would be creditable to the angler's skill under almost any circumstance of capture. I hazard the opinion, however, that they derive less real sport from their method than does the angler who fishes with a single dry and floating fly, imparts no motion to it, and presents an imitation of a natural insect which the trout is at liberty to inspect and, if his suspicion is aroused by the transparency of the fraud or because of some mistake in delivery, to reject. The dry fly angler must know quite as much of the haunts and habits of the fish as the wet fly angler and, to cast his fly successfully, must have the greater skill. Above all, the dry fly method is the more fascinating, because the angler actually sees the rise and the taking of the fly, the sense of sight as well as the sense of touch conducing to his pleasurable emotion. His imagination—all ardent anglers have imagination—will immediately come into play, and he will find himself convinced that the imitation has really deceived the fish into believing that a living insect lay upon the water.

I venture to suggest the fancy that the taking of a trout with a nondescript fly of blue or red—the Parmacheene Belle, the Jenny Lind, or what-not—even though it may have been presented accurately, superbly cocked and lightly floating, can never produce in the angler's mind the feeling of satisfaction that attends him when he captures a fine fish with a fair imitation of the natural fly upon the water at the time, or with one which may be assumed to represent in colour and form a natural fly of a species which might be expected to be about at the season. True, I may seem to be stretching the point too finely, but I have expressed the fancy to some of my friends, who, after hearing me, were good enough to say, as indeed I hoped they would, "Why, the trout that took the gaudy fly was a fool fish that would have taken anything." They seemed to believe, as I do, that the angler who captures a "fool" fish attains to no honour; that "fool" fish are not the sort of fish one should covet. The fancy may be strongly characterised by many as eccentric, I know, but I am sure that it embodies the principle and spirit of true sportsmanship.

The theory of imitation may not be justly attacked or lightly set aside because of the fact that nondescript flies frequently take fish,—sometimes after fair imitations have been refused. My own belief is that when the highly coloured nondescript is taken, success should be ascribed to the great skill of the angler and his particularly clean presentation of the fly, or to the fact that the fly was "popped" over and so close to a fish that it was seized because of its proximity.

The taking of trout with either of those two famous flies, the Gold-Ribbed Hare's Ear or the Wickham's Fancy, after fish have refused close imitations of the insects upon which they were feeding, might also be urged as an argument against the imitation theory, though against the colour part of it only, as those two patterns, while imitations, perhaps, of no individual insects, do bear a general resemblance to many, and may be said to be typical in form. It is quite possible that the bright tinsel body of the Wickham's Fancy, and the rib of gold wire or tinsel of the

Hare's Ear, represent to the trout that beautiful, iridescent colouring plainly visible upon the body of many natural insects. It is also quite possible that the flashing of the tinsel, opaque though it is, produces that quality of translucence so apparent in the natural insect.

The theory that a counterpart in colour and form of the natural food of the trout is more likely to prove effective than the nondescript, is logical, beyond question, not only because the imitation is likely to delude the fish, but also because of the appeal it makes to the angler's own sense of fitness; for it is more than likely that the angler, knowing his imitation to be a correct one, will feel a confidence that will enable him to make a cleaner presentation of it, and to simulate more closely the great essentials—action and position. And yet within the experience of every angler there have been times when the very closest imitation of the insect upon which the trout were presumably feeding, presented in the best possible manner, has failed to excite any interest on the part of the fish, and when an artificial in no way resembling the natural in colour took trout quite as well as the closest imitation. On such occasions the faith of the advocate of close imitation probably received a rude shock.

Although considered out of fashion among fly fishermen of the present day, one occasionally meets an angler who still adheres to what is known as the "routine" system. The advocates of this system believe in the necessity of presenting to the fish a certain series of artificial flies in February, another series in March, and continuing a different series for each month of the season. The theory is based, of course, upon the imitation of those insects which prevail in the particular months. "Routine" anglers of the past probably had opinions as firmly fixed as those of anglers of to-day, and it is very likely that there were a few who persistently clung to the prescribed flies for May, when fishing that month, and used no others—fish or no fish.

Whatever effect the colour of the artificial fly may have upon trout, and however necessary the proper shade may be felt to be when casting to fish that are feeding upon some particular species of insect, it is quite certain that the angler cannot rely upon this form of imitation alone to take fish. In fishing with the floating fly the imitation of the form of the natural insect, in my opinion, is quite as essential as that of its colour, and frequently size will be found to be even more important than either. My own experiences have convinced me that imitation of the natural insect is absolutely necessary, and I put the forms this should take in the following order—the order of their importance:

1st—Position of the fly upon the water.

2nd—Its action.

3rd—Size of the fly.

4th—Form of the fly.

5th—Colour of the fly.

The degrees of importance which separate form, size, and colour may not be widely marked, and, while an exact imitation of the colour, size, and form of the insect which the trout are taking is undoubtedly the ideal combination, I believe that if failure results from any variation from this combination, colour is least responsible for it.

I cannot go so far as to say that trout are entirely colour-blind, or that a correctly sized and shaped artificial dressed in blue would kill a fish that was taking a natural yellow dun, but I do believe that even a great divergence in the shade of colour of the artificial tied in imitation of the natural insect would make no material difference to the fish, if it were properly presented. In fact, it is my opinion that the artificial need not be yellow at all; that a fly of subdued colour—a Whirling Dun, a Silver Sedge, a Pink Lady, or any fly of similar conformation—will be accepted by the fish feeding upon a little Yellow May if its presentation is clean.

We have all had experience with certain fish, or, perhaps, with many fish, on certain days when, although they appeared to be feeding, it seemed next to impossible to induce a rise. Such failures are invariably ascribed to lack of proper imitation—usually, colour. Sometimes the angler, if he be an expert fly-tier, sets about fashioning a fly which resembles the insect some particular fish is taking, and presenting it either at that time or the next day, is delighted to find it taken readily. He is immediately a strong advocate of the theory of colour imitation, but he is sometimes uncertain that another pattern would not have served quite as well. Whether or not the pattern did the killing is really an open question.

Just above the dam in front of the Spruce Cabin Inn, at Canadensis, on the Brodhead, is a beautiful stretch of flat water where a great many fine fish may always be found. However, they are not always to be taken. Along the bank opposite the road, which at this point is but a few feet from the stream, is a heavy growth of wood. The rhododendron, which is quite thick, throws its roots out from the bank under water, and the interstices between these roots afford fine hiding-places for the fish. At the upper end of the wood, just where a field joins it, there is a deep hole which is the home of a very large trout—a fish that has sorely tried the patience of the few anglers who have attempted to take him. An overhanging tree prevents the delivery of a really effective cast from below, and this undoubtedly accounts for a great many failures. In three successive years I have raised this fish seven times (a very small proportion of the times I have tried for him), on four occasions leaving my fly with him, and not fastening solidly on the others. An old tree-stump to which the fish rushes immediately upon being hooked accounts for the smashes. The fish will not rise to a fly on coarse gut, and the fine gut will not hold him from the stump. If there ever was a trout that could convince the angler that exact—and even minute—imitation was absolutely essential, this is the one. He feeds regularly, and may be seen rising steadily for hours at a time. No amount of casting will put him down, unless clumsily done, and he will rise to a natural insect within a few inches of the artificial, time and again, ignoring the latter totally. On one occasion—the last time I tried for him—I failed so signally with all my favourite patterns, that I might have been convinced that exact imitation was necessary had it not been for the fact that the fish rose indiscriminately to many different sorts— spinners, gnats, and the smaller members of the beetle family, lady-bugs, and the like, and finally to an artificial

which bore no resemblance to any of these. I could not
imitate them all, and had tried faithfully with a fair imitation, in size and colour, of one species. It was all to no purpose, however, and to see him continually rising after the
many attempts I had made was, to say the least, chastening. I finally decided, after watching him feed for ten
minutes, to make one more attempt, and to keep casting
the one pattern until he took it or was put down. I knotted
on a fly known as the "Mole," which looks like an insect
on the water at a distance, but very unlike one when examined closely. This fly was offered probably twenty times or
more, without effect, the fish continuing to rise to the
natural insects all about it. The cast which eventually
raised him differed from any that I had previously made,
though without intent on my part. When the fly alighted
about a foot above the fish, it fell upon its side with one
wing on the surface and the other in the air. Drifting
down to within a few inches of the fish, it suddenly stood
erect and cocked, this apparently the result of some pressure brought to bear upon the leader by the slow current.
It had hardly assumed this upright position, and perhaps
was still in the act of regaining its equilibrium, when it disappeared and I was fast to the fish. He added this fly to
his collection, and while I sadly examined the leader to
ascertain the extent of the damage done, I was not wholly
discontented.

I threw a Whirling Dun to this fish one day over a
hundred times without putting him down or having him
evince the slightest interest in it. A few minutes later,
going up-stream from him, I detached the fly from the

leader, and, breaking the hook off at the bend, floated it down, and it was taken readily. Perhaps on this occasion I missed the psychological moment, and it is quite possible that the fly would have been taken if I had made one more cast, though not very probable. My own notion of it is that the pattern, when floated down with the hook broken off, had a certain naturalness which was lacking when it was attached to the leader. Either the leader itself was seen, or its restraint upon the fly destroyed its natural appearance. On the other hand, however, the difficulty in presenting the fly because of the overhanging tree may have prevented a proper presentation, though I think a great number of times it approached the fish admirably. Whatever the reason may have been, I did not rise him that day.

Perhaps the actions of another fish that I watched feeding steadily for over an hour may, while hardly offering a solution of the difficulty, present some basis for conjecture. A gentleman who had observed him feeding the day before called my attention to the fact that a good trout occupied a little pocket about one hundred yards above the big fish which has given me so much sport, and he led me mysteriously away from the inn, and as mysteriously up the road, until we reached the spot where the fish was, when he asked me to look in the little eddy and tell him what I saw. For a moment or two I could see nothing but a little drift stuff, but very shortly a good-sized snout broke the surface, and a large bubble floated where it had appeared. While we spent ten or fifteen minutes watching the fish rise, I laid plans to get him the next day. In the morning I thought better of it, however, and planned to crawl down to the water's edge and study his actions at close range. In clambering down the steep bank I was rather clumsy, and he took fright and disappeared. Getting as close as I could to the water, I hid behind a bush and watched for the fish to return, which he did in just four minutes, timed by my watch. This in itself was interesting, as it tended to show how long the incident lingered in his memory. The eddy which he occupied was formed at the bottom of a rather swift little run by a large boulder that deflected a part of the stream toward the bank and started it up-stream again. The fish stationed himself exactly in the centre of this up-stream current, which was not very strong, and immediately began feeding. He rose three or four times a minute, sometimes oftener, according to the opportunities presented. There were very few insects in the air, but apparently a great many upon the surface of the water. I think perhaps a half dozen or so of different sorts alighted directly in the eddy, all of which the fish accounted for, but the majority of rises were to insects that were carried down-stream upon the surface, and collected in the eddy. They were of all sizes and shapes, from the tiniest *Diptera*, which interested him much, to a small dead butterfly, lying flat, which he examined closely, but declined. It was this discrimination that puzzled me. He took many apparently dead insects, and refused many. He never refused any that were alive, and size or colour or shape made no difference to him. Why some dead insects appealed to him and others did not, I cannot guess, unless, perhaps, those that appeared dead to me, did not look so to him. Every time he rose, it was with the greatest deliberation; never did he rush at the fly, and once when a particularly active dun fluttered on the surface close to him, instead of rushing for it as I expected him to do, he merely backed up under it, rising very slowly, finally sucking it in. Another thing I noticed was that he never went forward to take an insect. He went forward frequently to meet one, but always took it backing up. This manner of taking a fly is not at all unusual, as fish may frequently be seen backing under an artificial, sometimes even turning down-stream before taking it. If an insect showed the slightest activity, which many of them did in various ways, moving the body up and down, opening and closing their wings, or moving their legs, he never hesitated, but took it at once, even the tiniest. If the insect lay upon its side, he would drift with it a foot or two, sometimes taking it, frequently leaving it. On one occasion he backed under an insect in this position for a distance of about three feet, and stopped, apparently abandoning it; but the next instant he turned, took it quietly, and swam slowly back to his station. I was unable to see this insect as clearly as I wished, and I do not know that it moved at the moment it was taken, but from the manner in which the fish took the others, it seems likely that this was the case. Notwithstanding the decided preference shown by this fish for the moving or living insects, he rose and took a piece of twig about three-eighths of an inch long which I flipped to him at a moment when he was unoccupied, and I found this twig in his stomach the next day, together with three spruce needles, two of which were green and one yellow. Would the presence of this drift stuff in his stomach indicate that the fish was near-sighted, or that such drift really had a place in his dietary?

I have found in the stomachs of trout many small sticks, plainly fresh, and which certainly formed no part of a caddis casing. Why they were taken is hard to say; some anglers have expressed the opinion, which may possibly be sound, that the fish are compelled to take them in the attempt to secure some poor shipwrecked insects which are using them as rafts. I prefer to believe, however, that they are mistaken by the fish for some form of life, perhaps having the appearance of caddis larvæ. The spruce needles were probably mistaken for willow flies, or some of the family of *Perlidæ*—those with wings that fold along the back.

That the fish was taken the following morning on the Mole, which certainly imitated no insect with which he may have been familiar, perhaps means nothing. As he was feeding regularly, and rather indiscriminately, he was probably an easy fish to take. The Mole was just another morsel that looked natural enough. The first cast took him, the fly drifting up to him after having been cast over the boulder at the bottom of the eddy. The leader was not seen, and as the fly appeared in a natural, upright position, his suspicion was not aroused, and a minute or two later he was in the net. Withal, the fish showed a decided preference for living insects, and refused those which were certainly no deader than an artificial fly; and yet the Mole was taken with just as much confidence as if it had been a living thing. I think it quite within reason that any pattern of fly properly presented would have taken the fish as readily as did the fly which he rose to, and my conclusion is that it was because of its position that it was taken. My observation of this fish confirmed my belief in the necessity of so placing the fly that it would come to the fish just as a natural insect would, floating upon the surface. There is a great difference between the effect produced by a fly cast upon likely looking water, or to a feeding fish, without special care as to where it may alight, and that produced by one cast exactly to the proper spot.

The larger fish down-stream apparently was interested only in live insects, which is shown, I think, by his utter refusal of every artificial of any pattern, including the Mole, which he ignored each time it came over him, until the twist in the leader, or some other uncontrolled action, turned the fly over on the surface, and simulated to a certain extent the struggle of an insect endeavoring to rise from the water. I am convinced that my many failures with this fish were due, in the main, to my inability to place the fly in a proper position. This conclusion is supported, I think, by the fact that he took the unattached Whirling Dun—which I was careful to float down to him in the proper current—after he had refused it scores of times when attached to the leader.

CHAPTER VI

SOME FANCIES—SOME FACTS

SOME anglers have come to believe that the trout of our heavily fished streams have developed such wariness and cunning that they view the artificial fly of the angler with suspicion, even if they do not actually know it to be an imitation, In the light of certain experiences of my own, I am unable to concur in the conclusion reached by these anglers that trout are capable of reasoning or remembering specific incidents for any long period of time; it is my opinion—presented, however, with some hesitancy—that they refuse the artificial fly not because they have had previous experience with it but because of various other reasons, the most important of which are the unnatural *action* of the fly, and the probability of the fish having seen the angler, his rod, the leader, or the shadow of one or all. Surely the trout of these streams cannot in July and August remember the hordes of anglers that invaded their haunts in May. Admitting it to be true that in the earlier months of the season it is comparatively easy to take trout, even when the streams are full of anglers, and that later, in the summer months, with but two or three anglers, or at most a half dozen, to be seen, infinite skill is often required to induce even a single fair rise,

128

something other than the memory of the fish must be the cause of his reluctance to rise, as the following instances may tend to prove.

In July, 1911, I rose, hooked, and returned to the water four fish three times each in one week; and these fish were taken in the same place and on the same pattern of fly each time. On another occasion I rose and landed an eleven-inch rainbow trout which I returned to the water, and the next day this fish was brought home by a fellow angler who had taken him in the same place. This last may possibly have been another fish; but about the four other trout there can be no mistake, as I marked them without injury before returning them to the water the first time. I was prompted to make this experiment after taking a fish from one spot, which resembled closely in size and form a fish I had returned to the water a few days previously. This fish was one of the four, and was twice taken and returned. Each of the fish gave up a minute piece of its caudal fin in return for its life.

Often, too, one hears of trout being taken with the fly of some luckless or careless angler fast in its jaw. On the Brodhead, in 1907, one morning about eight o'clock, I rose and killed a native trout weighing about a pound, which had a fly in its lip left there by an angler the evening before; his nose was raw and bleeding where he had scraped it against the stones in his efforts to dislodge the hook. Experiences of this sort do not tend to confirm the belief that fish have memory.

The more enemies an animal has the more wary it is, and in those least able to defend themselves against attack the senses which enable them to avoid danger are most keen. In some animals, sight, smell, and hearing are all keenly alert; in others a combination of two of these senses is relied upon, and in rare cases but one. These faculties give warning of the approach of an enemy, and time, in most cases, for the use of such secondary means of defence as are provided by nature—speed, flight, protective colouring, or whatever they may be.

In the case of trout, since scientists have come to no definite conclusion that fish can smell, we may safely assume—from the fly fisher's standpoint, at any rate—that this sense has no place in our study. The same may be said of taste and feeling; the luckless fish relying upon these senses would find himself hard and fast before he could reach the conclusion that the feathered fly was not what it appeared to be. This leaves sight and hearing as the means by which the trout is apprised of the approach of danger—and the angler may well say that they are quite sufficient.

> "If fish could hear as *well* as see,
> Never a fisher would there be."

The experiments made by Ronalds and described in his "Fly Fishers' Entomology" prove more or less conclusively that trout cannot hear, or at least are not disturbed by sounds produced in the air. Now, while it is quite certain that they are affected by vibrations communicated to the water, the bottom of the stream, or its banks, I do not believe that the disturbance is conveyed to the senses of the fish unless the vibrations take place close to it. In this connection, an experiment made by myself may prove interesting, even though it may be in no way conclusive, as it was tried but once, and the trout which served as the medium may have been "deaf." Taking my position on a high bank above the fish and completely out of sight, I had a young man go below and thirty feet down-stream. Lying prone upon the opposite shore, which was level with the water, and taking pains not to make any quick move which might have spoiled the experiment, he took two stones, one in each hand, and, at a signal from me, struck them together, a foot under water. He did this a dozen times, each succeeding blow being harder than the previous one. The sound produced by the clashing stones had no apparent effect upon the fish, but I noticed that the series of small waves or ripples created by the disturbance of the surface, upon reaching the trout, seemed to make it uneasy, and it began "weaving" from side to side, covering, however, not more than a foot in its movements. When the fish had quieted down, and after another trial, with the same effect, I had the lad abandon the stones and make as large a wave as he could, directed toward the fish. There was considerable splashing during the attempt, but the trout gave no indication that it was aware of the disturbance until the first ripple was passing over it, when it became as uneasy as before, and even more excited; and not until the ripple had ceased did it resume the almost stationary position previously held. The fish was about one foot from the surface, and the largest ripple not over two inches in height; consequently, its motion could hardly have been felt at a depth greater than six inches; yet the fish was disturbed—whether by the action of the water itself or by the shadow cast by the ripple, I leave for the reader to decide. Of one thing I am positive: the fish was not disturbed by the sound of the colliding stones.

The fish's sense of sight is so keen that it alone enables the trout to avoid danger, and is absolutely necessary to its existence. But it is not so keen, in my opinion, as to enable the trout to detect minute differences between the angler's fly and the natural insect—except, of course, when the action of the artificial fly is so unnatural as to warn the fish, or frighten it.

Adherents to the theory that trout are able to distinguish between the angler's artificial fly and the natural insect, make much of the admitted fact that a fish is rarely taken from the much fished Southern streams on a Parmacheene Belle or other nondescript. There is a great deal of truth in the contention; but the fact is lost sight of that these flies are usually presented by anglers who have but little knowledge of the habits of the fish they are seeking, their experience having been gained solely at the expense of the trout of the wilderness.

While not asserting the opinion that a gaudy fly will not take fish, I would remind the reader that such a fly is usually cast by a man who presents himself to the fish before he offers the fly—with the inevitable result. The instinct of self-preservation is strong in the trout, and he flees the apparition, though, if he would but realise it, he was never safer than at the very moment of its appearance.

Anything unusual that comes within the vision of the fish means to him a possible danger, and the desire to feed, if he be in the mood, is forgotten in his effort to locate the point of attack. Any shadow thrown upon the water indicates the approach of an enemy—a heron, a kingfisher, a mink (the most destructive of all), or a man, in whom he recognises an enemy only because he sees a moving object. Beset as the trout is at all times, it is but natural that he should make use of his only means of defence—speed— and escape while he may. On streams that are much fished, frequent sight of man is afforded the fish, and, although the actions of the angler (except in rare cases) do not indicate the danger of actual personal encounter, the fish retires, precipitately or quietly, according to the manner in which he is approached. It is this sight of man or his shadow, and not the ability to detect the fraud, that impels him to refrain from taking the fly. If the angler remains hidden from view, and throws the fly properly, without the accompaniment of shadows of himself, rod, line, or leader, and a rise is not induced, he may safely assume that it is lack of inclination on the part of the fish, and not a contempt for the pattern of the fly, bred of familiarity with it, that causes him to refuse it.

These facts, or fancies, as they may be considered, are presented only as they may support a theory that accounts for the wariness and cunning of the trout of much fished streams, and the apparent lack of these attributes in the trout of the wilderness. It is a well known fact that a man who wishes to take trout in Maine, Quebec, New Brunswick, Nova Scotia, or, in fact, anywhere in the North Woods where they are plentiful, need have had no previous experience to enable him to catch all that the law, or his conscience permits. This same man fishing in Pennsylvania or lower New York, practising the same methods he applied in the North, will leave the streams with the idea firmly fixed in his mind that they are barren of fish, or, perchance, viewing the catch made by a more skilful angler, will come to the conclusion that the fish are more wary than their fellows of the North, and that a skill unknown to the angler lacking experience on these waters is required to take them. The instinct of self-preservation is quite as strong in the trout of the wilderness, but expresses itself in other ways that are in keeping with the different conditions they have to contend with.

In most places where trout are plentiful, there is abundance of room for them to escape from an enemy, an advantage denied the trout which are restricted to the narrow confines of one of our mountain streams, particularly when the water is low and the trout have to be more wary than ever, if they are to survive. While endowed with the same agility and the same keenness of sight, the wilderness fish are emboldened by numbers, and appear to depend a great deal upon one another for warning; they are alert only to the "main chance," *i. e.*, the taking of anything that looks like food. This explains why it is easy for the veriest tyro fishing in the wilderness to take as many fish with the fly in a single day as the expert on the Southern streams would be content to take in a season. Many of these big catches are made upon lakes and streams that are heavily fished, yet the angler rarely has to resort to methods which require any great skill. In many instances the fishing is done from a canoe, and fish are taken quite close to it, the interest on the part of the trout seemingly being actuated by nothing more than a desire to "beat his fellows to it."

The law of "the survival of the fittest" applies equally to the fish of the Southern streams and to the fish of the wilderness. In both cases vigilance and agility are the price of continued existence—on the one hand, to avoid the attack which may deprive the fish of life, on the other, to excel in the scramble for that which will sustain it.

If the old saw which runs, "When the wind is in the north the skilful fisherman goes not forth," etc., referred to fly fishing, it was plainly meant for the angler who did not care to indulge in his sport when the chilling blasts from this quarter were howling about the stream, because it is in no sense descriptive of the effect of the wind upon the feeding of the fish. When an angler has taken trout under conditions ranging from flat calms to gales from every point of the compass, it is difficult for him to believe that wind has any direct effect upon the fish, aside, perhaps, from the influence it exerts in promoting or retarding the development of the insects upon which they feed; and this last depends more upon the temperature of the wind than it does upon its force or the quarter from which it comes.

The angler who is fishing the flat, still water of a pond or lake hopes for a breeze in order that he may take advantage of the ripple caused by it, and deceive or approach his fish more readily. The advantage afforded by the breeze is offset on many occasions, in proportion to the force of the wind, by the increased difficulty of casting; and when a stiff wind is blowing down-stream or in the face of the

angler it is of negligible value. So far as comfort is concerned, a chilling wind is very disagreeable, and the angler
unfortunate enough to be upon the stream during a
"norther" in the early spring is quite of the mind that trout
are sensible of it, when he finds them in no keener mood
for the sport than he is; yet it was on just such a day, as cold
and blustering as I have ever experienced, that the trout
on the Brodhead, of which I have told, rose to the fly
which was made to play such pranks by the wind.

There is a gentleman of my acquaintance, an expert with
the fly, who holds that it is useless to fish a wooded stream
when the wind is blowing heavily, not so much because
of any change in atmospheric conditions, but because the
rapidly moving shadows thrown upon the water by the
frantically waving overhead limbs and branches seem to
make the trout restless or nervous and unwilling to feed.
Be this as it may, it certainly does not apply upon the open
stretches, for there the wind is of distinct advantage, because the ruffled surface helps to conceal the angler's
activities from the fish. When success does not attend the
caster's efforts on days of this sort, failure must be ascribed
to his state of mind rather than to the condition of the
weather.

And here just a hint from my own experience: beware
of fishing in big woods on a very windy day; dead limbs
may come crashing down at any moment. On one occasion
a difference of ten feet in my position would have meant
disaster and these pages might never have been written.

During periods of high wind the trout are often treated
to a change of diet, land flies, grasshoppers, and beetles,

unhappily overcome, being readily and cheerfully accepted. On one occasion, all the trout killed by five or six anglers disclosed the fact, upon autopsy, that potato-bugs had formed a large part of their food that morning; and a fly which resembled this beetle only in size and shape was found very effective. This fly was a herl-bodied brown palmer, called the Marlow Buzz.

The many anglers who still hold to the belief that trout will not rise during a thunder-storm do so, no doubt, because it offers an excuse for retiring from the stream and seeking shelter,—for which they cannot be blamed. It is not the pleasantest situation to be caught in one of the vicious storms which sometimes break with scant warning. If, however, it happens that the angler is so placed that he is far from a road or path that will lead him to some cover, he is far safer in the stream than in the woods; and, making the best of a bad bargain, he should continue his fishing. In all likelihood, he will come to the conclusion that the theory is not founded upon fact; for, while trout do not invariably rise during thunder-storms, they may be taken on occasions when the reverberations are so heavy as to be felt almost as distinctly as they are heard—the effect upon the fish not being apparent.

If the storm be accompanied by a heavy rain, dry fly fishing ceases as soon as the water begins to rise and becomes discoloured, because, even though the fish may be ready to feed, there is small likelihood of the angler's fly being seen by them through the discoloured water. But no time should be wasted in returning to the stream after the flood has run off and the water is clearing, as the opportunity for taking fish is then probably the best that will be presented.

Idiosyncrasy—or shall we call it superstition?—seems to enter into the make-up of a great many anglers.

Squire Jake Price, now dead, father of the boys who keep that comfortable hostelry on the Brodhead, at Canadensis, in Pennsylvania, well known to many anglers, was famous as a trout fisherman. He fished with the fly only, tied his own flies, and from the time his sons were able to wade the streams would permit them to use nothing else. Always keen to be at his fishing, he would not be dragged to the waterside unless his "almanac" told him the time was propitious. Curiously enough, when he did go, he always took fish; but this may be ascribed to the fact that he "knew how" rather than to a revelation from the zodiac.

A story is told of an angler of indifferent skill, but anxious to take home a basket of fish, who induced Squire Jake to accompany him one morning. He felt certain of getting trout, the Squire having approved of the day. Upon their arrival at the stream-side he proceeded to line his creel with fine grasses and ferns, when, to his amazement, the Squire left abruptly, saying he could not fish with one who would thus "fly in the face of Providence." Was this superstition, or only anger at the other's assurance?

Of similar mind to the Squire are those anglers who persist in carrying, to their own inconvenience, a diminutive creel and smaller net, preferring to cram into either a fish twice too large rather than to carry equipment of adequate size; the taking of a good fish is a circumstance which they feel may never be realised if they anticipate it.

Some consideration must be given to the belief of those who have unbounded faith in a particular pattern of fly. There are wet fly fishermen on the Beaverkill who never make up their cast of three flies without including the Royal Coachman; and at least one of these, whom I know, uses this fly, dry, in preference to any other. While the pattern has no place in my book, I respect the faith others have in it, which faith, however, is often rudely shaken— for a short period, at least. After fishing carefully for hours with his favourite fly without response, the angler meets a brother angler who displays two or three nice fish taken on the Queen, the Bumble, or what not, and passes on. For the nonce the favourite is discarded, the Queen or Bumble is knotted on, but the result is the same—nothing. Another pattern is tried—same result. Again the fly is changed, and again, and still again. In his anxiety our friend uses little skill, less judgment, and lacks entirely the great essential— faith.

Many times an angler, stepping quietly into the stream at the beginning of his day's sport, casts his fly to a spot where his experience tells him a trout may be, and meets with response almost immediately. His next cast is accepted quite as quickly, and in these few delicious moments, with the nucleus in his creel, the vision he has had of the one great day's catch begins to take tangible form. But how rudely the vision is dissipated in the next four or five hours, during which time he gets not a single rise!

There are other anglers in whom entirely different emotions are aroused when they are successful in taking fish soon after their arrival at the stream. To them this incident spells utter failure for the rest of the day. It seems to me that these men neglect to analyse the situation, permitting superstition to run riot with reason, and, to my mind, their troubles may be ascribed to any one of three causes: (1) At the time the angler first steps into the stream he may be arriving at the top or at the end of a rise that started fifteen, twenty, or thirty minutes before, which short space of time may be responsible for the difference between two fish and a possible half dozen. If the angler meets with this experience during the season when the water is very low and clear, and the day hot and bright, he may be satisfied that, to a great extent, such is the explanation. But, if he is not a principal to cause number two, he should be able to continue taking some trout, even under these trying conditions. (2) The optimist arriving at the stream side prepares his rod, surveys the scene of action, and, having selected the spot he is to fish, enters the stream some distance below, and quietly proceeds to his point of vantage. Every instinct alert, he is careful to make no mistake, and his care and deftness are at once rewarded. Continuing a few yards, another fish is taken, and possibly a bit farther on, still another. Then, blinded by conceit, he falls into the pit he has dug for himself. He thinks he has at last the right medicine, and unknowingly (and unmeaningly, bless his heart) there steals over him a feeling akin to contempt for the wary fish he is after. The next pool is approached with a swagger that fills the trout that inhabit it with consternation, and drives all thought of feeding from them. Some day it will occur to this angler that he has been a bit overconfident, and he will try getting out of the stream, going up a hundred yards through the brush, and starting all over as at the beginning; then he will come to a realisation of the truth. (3) The pessimist, by analysing cause number two, may overcome, to a certain extent, the deep-rooted superstition that, because he gets a trout easily at the outset, he will get no more throughout the day. His is a state of mind that surely is not conducive to best effort. After taking a fish on the first few casts, his subsequent proceedings are governed by an anomalous condition of mind—he believes that his sport is over, yet hopes the day may prove the fallacy of his theory, and, in an unconscious effort to avoid his fate, he fishes in a careless manner.

The rise which indicates that a large fish is feeding has, upon the minds of some anglers, a psychological effect which works toward defeating any attempt they make in throwing to him. The angler is alert only to the necessity of placing his fly near the fish, and, caution thrown to the winds, he approaches in a manner which might be called stealthy if he used it in escaping from a burning building. Having begun without caution, thus preparing the way to dismal failure, he fixes his eye upon the spot where the rise was noted, and sends his fly, with no thought, perhaps, other than to get it on the water as quickly as possible. If his efforts meet with no reward—and the chances are they will not—and many fish are to be seen feeding all about, he probably becomes frantic with desire to take one, runs through a rapid change of flies in the hope of finding one that will entice, wastes many precious minutes in his fum-

bling uncertainty, when suddenly all rising ceases, and he
has lost his opportunity.

The remedy for all of these cases is the same—calmness
and deliberation.

The suggestion that the sight of the leader is abhorrent
to trout brings up a point upon which great stress is laid
by dry fly anglers. That the fish is warned off by seeing
the gut upon the surface of low, clear water is to my mind
more certain than anything else in the sport of angling.
Whether or not frequent sight of the leader makes the fish
familiar with it, is difficult to determine. Personally, I believe that when a fish refuses a fly because he has seen the
leader attached to it, his timidity is likely to be due to the
impression of its unnaturalness at the moment, rather than
to his recollection of having seen a like object before and
learned its danger. In plain words—probably inviting a
storm of protest and criticism—I am not inclined to the
notion that trout become "educated" on streams that are
much fished. These trout are quite sensitive to danger, but,
in my opinion, only imminent danger affects them. The
sudden appearance of an angler waving a rod, or of a cow
fording the stream, are disturbing to trout, one just as
much as the other. Both angler and cow are in motion,
and that alone attracts the eye of the fish; both intercept
light, and thus cast shadows upon the water, which mean
possible danger to him.

Anything falling upon the surface of the water arouses
interest on the part of a fish observing it; if it be a shadow,
he suspects danger in proportion to its size and activity;
the fall of a leaf, a twig, or an insect is interesting to him

in one way or another. Frequently a leaf or twig, if not so large as to frighten him at once, will be investigated at close range. I have thrown maple buds to trout, which were taken almost immediately upon striking the water, being slowly ejected afterward when it was discovered that the buds were not food.

An insect intercepts light, but the insignificant shadow it casts does not alarm the fish, and his attention is directed to the insect alone. When the artificial fly is thrown, however, it must necessarily be with the leader attached, and if it so happens that the leader, or that part of it close to the fly, *floats upon the surface,* the attention of the fish is divided between the fly itself and the leader, the latter standing out boldly between the eye of the fish and the background of sky. The leader floating upon the surface is more visible to the fish than when fully submerged. The angler who wishes to demonstrate this may do so by placing a length of gut upon the surface of some still, sunlit water, noting the shadow cast by it upon the bed of the stream, and then comparing it with the shadow of the same gut submerged.

The water-strider, skipping nimbly over the surface of clear, shallow water, affords an excellent illustration of shadow effects. The shadows thrown upon the bottom by this curious insect are enormous when compared with its actual size, and those resulting from the depression in the surface made by the insect's feet look to be as big as a dime. It was observation of the shadows thrown by the water-strider that prompted me to experiment with the leader; and my first attempt, made with the lightest leader

I had, produced a shadow upon the bottom *nearly an inch in width.* Whether or not this shadow alarms the fish more than does the leader itself, probably depends upon the circumstances controlling the direction of his attention at the time, but it is certain that one or the other does have a marked effect upon his behaviour. Perhaps both combined have, and, consequently, he can hardly be expected to take the fly when his interest is divided betwixt the desire to feed, on the one hand, and suspicion tinged with fear on the other.

Upon glassy water, the glistening leader, twisting and turning upon the surface, accompanied by little wrinkles along its entire length, presents to the fish an aspect which must at least arouse his curiosity and distract his attention from the fly—even though it does not terrify him and scare him off entirely.

The visibility of the leader has always been one of the problems of the fly fisher, irrespective of the question of drag. Many attempts have been made to produce a leader of neutral colour that would be invisible, or approximately so, when on the water. I have done some experimenting in this direction myself. I have tried all colours—greens and browns, mist colours and greys. I have steeped leaders in ink until they came out absolutely black. Yet, withal, I have failed to satisfy myself that one was better than the others, when I came to use it on the stream. If there is one colour that a leader may be stained to render it less visible than another, I do not know what it is. I am inclined to believe, however, that gut of natural colour is less conspicuous than gut that has been coloured to make it harmonise with the water. Partial solutions of the problem may be had by assuming certain controlling conditions to exist. For instance, as the fish views the leader from below, and against a background formed by the sky, a light-blue leader to harmonise with the background on a bright day, or, for a similar reason, a grey one on a cloudy day, may be the very thing. Of course, it is all very speculative, because the main element of the problem—what the fish thinks—is an unknown one.

In my opinion, the floating, drifting leader, with its wrinkles and its convolutions, constitutes the worst possible form of drag, which must be avoided if trout are to be taken where the water is slow and unruffled. The angler should endeavour to have the fly float and the leader sink—obviously, by keeping one *dry* and the other *wet*. He will find it even more difficult to keep the leader wet than to keep the fly dry; even when thoroughly saturated, the former will not submerge readily when the fly is thrown as lightly as it should be.

In swifter water it is easier to keep the leader under the surface, but here one encounters another form of drag which, while in my opinion not so fatal to the angler's chances as the one I have described, is oftentimes more exasperating. This form of drag takes place when the fly, although accurately and lightly placed in the desired spot, is snatched away almost at once by the current pulling on the line or leader; the fish may thus be deprived of an opportunity of securing the fly, or he may refuse it because of its unnatural action. The natural insect, unhampered by any "string to it," drifts naturally with the current, and the feeding fish which makes for it, having accurately judged its position and pace, rarely misses. The artificial, when drag is exerted upon it, dashes down-stream at a speed always greater than that of the current in which it is; besides the unnatural action it acquires, it sometimes ceases to be a floating fly, being dragged under the surface by the pull of the line or leader in the swifter water. Drag of this sort usually occurs when the line or the leader must fall on the swift water between the angler and the spot he desires to reach with the fly, and is not always avoidable. Where possible, the line and leader should be kept out of the swift water.

When casting to the eddies at the head of a pool, the angler should assume a position on the same side of the current as the eddy to be fished. An effort should be made to place the line in the water that is turning *up-stream* where the eddy begins to take form. The fly falling farther up will remain floating for a time—quite long enough to be taken by a fish. If this eddy cannot be reached from directly below, because of the depth of water or on account of some obstacle to clean casting, the fly may be thrown across the current with the up-stream curve in the leader. Where this is found necessary the leader should be watched carefully and, before it begins to exert a pull on the fly, the latter should be retrieved quickly. The fly may be taken from the water quietly, as it should be, if a forward loop is thrown in the line similar to that used in the switch cast. This action removes the leader from the water with but little disturbance, and as the fly is about to leave the surface, the backward cast will carry it clear, practically without commotion. In the same manner an eddy across stream may be fished with little danger of a fish being put down by the sight of a dragging fly. The method, however, calls for keen alertness, and the angler must have perfect and constant control of rod and line.

Swift water in either a rift or a run should have no terrors for the angler who fears a dragging fly, if he will first study the currents. Even if he feels that a fish is occupying water that can be reached only by risking drag, he must always bear in mind that a fish is more likely to come some distance to a natural-looking fly than it is to take an unnatural one close to it. A spot should be selected as close to the assumed position of the fish as possible; but this choice should always be guided by the necessity for placing the fly on water swifter than that in which the line and leader will fall. The "retarded" drag which may set in after the fly has been placed in swift water, has floated downstream until it is below the leader, and is held back by it, need not be feared, because the fly will have covered a considerable stretch in its travel, and may then be retrieved. Sometimes the sight of a dragging fly is more offensive to the angler than it is to the fish; and there are occasions when it will be taken, if its actions have not been particularly rude.

As an aid to keeping the line afloat in swift water, an application of deer's fat, or one of the many preparations now made for the same purpose, is recommended. It is sufficient to treat three or four yards at the end of the line, and the dressing should be rubbed down smoothly afterward. Under no circumstances should any dressing be applied to the leader, because, even though it helps to float the fly, the gut will be found to be annoyingly buoyant when the still reaches are being fished, and will produce that troublesome form of drag already described, and which I consider the only form that unduly taxes the ingenuity and patience of the expert and even-tempered. My own opinion is that the sight of the leader does not seriously deter the fish from taking the fly in swift water. But on smooth water a super-buoyant leader is a nuisance and a plague and an abomination.

CHAPTER VII
THE POINT OF VIEW

THE capture of a splendid ouananiche under circumstances most trying is somewhere described by a well-known writer, who, in his inimitable style, exhibits himself before his readers running through his entire assortment of artificial flies, first one and then another and still another, and all without avail. We see him casting, casting, all impatience, determined, perhaps exasperated. Surely some sort of lure is predicated. But what? Ah, he has it! A live grasshopper. Then follows the pursuit, the overtaking, and the capture of the grasshopper, the impaling of its unfortunate body, its proffer to the fish, a desperate battle, and, finally, the contemplation of the finest fish of the season safely landed. The thrilling moment! Which was it? Why, of all moments, that one in which he captured the grasshopper! The story affords a fine illustration of what I call the "point of view," but until after the revelation that came to me with my first success with the dry fly, I did not fully appreciate its finer and deeper meanings.

A certain pleasurable excitement always attends the taking of a good fish by the true angler. Yet, after all, the quality of his gratification should be measured by the method of capture. In angling, as in all other arts, one's taste and discrimination develop in proportion to his opportunity to see, study, and admire the work of greater artists. Even as a knowledge of the better forms of music leads, eventually, to a distaste for the poorer sorts, and as familiarity with the work of great painters leads to disgust with the chromo-lithograph-like productions of the dauber, so, too, does a knowledge of the higher and more refined sorts of angling lead just as surely to the ultimate abandonment of the grosser methods. One who has learned to cast the fly seldom if ever returns to the days when he was content to sit upon the bank, or the string-piece of a pier, dangling his legs overboard while he watched his cork bobbing up and down, indicating by its motions what might be happening to the bunch of worms at the hook end of the line; and, even as casting the fly leads to the abandonment of the use of bait, so, too, does the dry fly lead to the abandonment of the wet or sunk fly. There can be no question but that the stalking of a rising trout bears to the sport of angling the same relation to its grosser forms as the execution of a symphony bears to the blaring of the local brass band. It appeals to the higher and more æsthetic qualities of the mind, and dignifies the pot-hunter's business into an art of the highest and finest character.

I am thus brought to the consideration of the pot-hunter and the fish hog. Many angling writers there be who have not hesitated, nor have they been ashamed, to describe the taking of great numbers of trout on separate and many occasions. They feel, no doubt, that such narratives entitle them to consideration as authorities on the subject. I quote from one—who shall be nameless—his bragging description of a perfect slaughter of fish. After telling of twenty-five or thirty trout taken during midday, naming at least a dozen flies he had found *killing,* he concludes: "All my trout were taken from the hook and *thrown twenty-five* feet to shore. Thirty, my friend claimed, yet when I came to count tails I found *forty* as handsome trout as ever man wished to see, and all caught from six in the evening until dark, about seven forty-five. I had no net or creel, therefore had to lead my trout into my hand. The friend at whose house I was staying claims I lost more than I caught by having them flounder off the hook *while trying to take them by the gills and by flinging them ashore.*" The italics are mine. And this fellow had the temerity to add that some poor devil (an itinerant parson, he called him) annoyed him by wading in and fishing with a "stick cut from the forest." Had Washington Irving witnessed this fellow's fishing I doubt that he would have been moved to write: "There is certainly something in angling that tends to produce a gentleness of spirit and a pure serenity of mind."

There are men calling themselves anglers—save the mark!—who limit the number of fish to the capacity of creel and pockets, and to whom size means merely compliance with the law—a wicked law, at that, which permits the taking of immature trout. It is not an inspiring sight to see a valiant angler doing battle with a six-inch trout, and, after brutally subjecting it to capture, carefully measuring it on the butt of his rod which he has marked for the purpose, stretching it, if necessary, to meet the law's requirements, and in some cases, if it does not come up to the legal standard, rudely flinging it away in disgust—to die as a result of its mishandling. Happily, this tribe is not increasing, because of the persistent efforts of true sportsmen who do not hesitate to denounce it publicly whenever opportunity arises. Perhaps it is permissible to hope that the pot-hunter and the fish hog may in time disappear, but, if this desirable end is to be brought about, true sportsmen must not shun their duty but must wage unceasing war against them.

Books on angling abound in word-pictures descriptive of the strenuous battle of the hooked fish to escape its captor, many such pictures being so vividly drawn that the reader fairly imagines himself in the writer's waders, his excitement ending only when the captive is in the net. It is meet, therefore, that some consideration be given to the point of view of those anglers who believe that great merit attaches to him who lands a good fish on light tackle.

There can be no question of the excitement attending the playing of a good trout nor of the skill required in its handling, and this excitement, in proportion to the ideas of the individual, is a greater or less measure of the sport; but, given the opportunity, it is my opinion that, in the hands of a skilful angler, the rod will kill nine out of ten fish hooked. Be that as it may, can the degree of skill, even with the lightest tackle, displayed in the landing of a two or three pound trout (a fine fish on our Eastern streams) bear comparison with that required in the capture of a six-foot tarpon on a six-ounce rod and a six-strand line? A six-foot tarpon will weigh about one hundred and twenty pounds, and the line will bear a deadweight strain of twelve pounds. Compare this with the three-pound trout taken on a gut leader, the weakest link in the angler's chain, which will lift a weight of two or more pounds, and the futility of beguiling oneself with the belief that the trout has any advantage will be apparent.

The playing of a trout is undeniably part of the sport, but, however difficult one wishes to make it, it is but secondary to the pleasure derived from casting the fly and deluding that old trout into mistaking it for a bit of living food. It is this art, this skill, this study of the fish itself and its habits, that places dry fly fishing for trout far ahead of all other forms of angling. It has been said that there is no sport that requires in its pursuit a greater knowledge of the game, more skill, more perseverance, than fly fishing, and that no sport holds its votaries longer. I am quite of this opinion. "There is no genuine enjoyment in the easy achievement of any purpose," and in fly fishing a full measure of satisfaction is obtained only when the taking of a single fish is accomplished under conditions most difficult and trying.

The true angler is content only when he feels that he has taken his fish by the employment of unusual skill. The highest development of this skill at the present state of the angler's art is the dry fly method. I do not deny that there are many anglers who have carried sunk fly and even worm casting to a high degree of specialisation and refinement; yet it seems to me—nay, more than that, it is a positive conviction with me—that no manner of sunk fly or worm or bait casting bears any sort of favourable comparison to the dry fly. I know that in this country, at least, the dry fly man is accused by his sunk fly fellows of being affected, dogmatic, fanatic. Yet it is not so. The dry fly man has passed through all of the stages of the angler's life, from the cane pole and the drop-line to the split bamboo and the fur-and-feather counterfeit of the midge fly. He has experienced throes of delight each time he advanced from the lower to the higher grade of angler. I insist that I do not make my words too strong when I say that in all of angling there is no greater delight than that which comes to the dry fly angler who simulates a hatch of flies, and entices to the surface of the water a fish lying hidden, unseen, in the stronghold of his own selection. Let him who doubts put aside his prejudice long enough to give the premier method fair trial, and soon he will be found applying for the highest degree of the cult—"dry fly man."

CHAPTER VIII

A FEW PATTERNS OF FLIES

T HE literature devoted to the subject of the artificial fly is very extensive and informing, and it is not my intention to add thereto except for the purpose of describing a few flies that I use in my own fishing. The tackle shops offer almost countless patterns of flies of varied hues and forms, and anglers can indulge their individual tastes by choosing sizes, colours, and shapes to suit their fancies. I have never attempted to compute the number of artificial flies listed in the dealers' catalogues and described in the works of angling writers, but I think it must run into the hundreds. There is, however, a growing tendency toward restriction in the number of special patterns used in actual fishing, and in my own fishing I have reduced this number to a very small one.

It is doubtless true that the fly fisher derives no small part of his pleasure from the act of selecting and purchasing flies. It is within the experience of every fly fisher, I think, that, under the influence of the memory of a certain fish taken on a particular pattern of fly, he includes a dozen or two of the sort in his next purchase. Perhaps the fly is a nondescript that he may never again find successful, but, nevertheless, he adds it to his store. Angling friends rec-

155

ommend their patterns to him, or some special flies they found taking under certain circumstances or over particular streams, and these, too, he buys and puts away. Maybe he may never use one of them, and in the end he comes, perhaps, to feel, as does the philatelist, great pleasure in the possession of a worthy collection: he has the pride of ownership, but no thought of putting his treasures to use. Of course, there can be no reasonable objection to fly collecting, and I can see how it may become as fascinating an employment as stamp or coin collecting.

Assuming that the angler is a believer in close imitation, he will, of course, be content only when he has all the patterns which have been created by the votaries of the theory; but if he should be inclined to agree with me— that a great part of the imitation must be produced by the angler himself while actually fishing the stream—he will find that about ten patterns will suffice under nearly all circumstances.

I give the dressings of eight patterns, although I rarely use over six. If I were compelled to do so, I could get along very well with one—the Whirling Dun. Fishing the Brodhead throughout the month of July, I used this fly exclusively, and took fish every day except two. On three separate occasions I used a different fly—at one time a Pink Lady, at another a Mole, and at still another a Silver Sedge. On each occasion I took one fish with the selected fly, after which I went back to the Whirling Dun, and continued my fishing. I killed one or two fish each day, the average for the month being very close to a pound and a half. I returned many fish to the water, and these averaged over ten inches. Some days the fish were feeding, and some days they were not. There was apparently little difference in the taking effect of the fly, except that it was taken readily when it was delivered properly, and never when it was not.

No matter how great the faith an angler has in a single pattern, it will naturally be very difficult for him to confine himself to its exclusive use. So much of his sport depends upon its delightful uncertainty, that if he does confine himself to the use of the single pattern, he will, of a consequence, be denied the pleasure of congratulating himself upon the acumen he has shown by the selection of the fly which is taken, after the favourite has been refused.

With the exception of the Pink Lady, the flies described are all standard patterns—tied, however, according to my own preference. Anglers who wish a more varied choice, one that includes one or two fancies, may add to the list a Wickham's Fancy and, for use when the fish are smutting, a small black gnat tied with a glossy black hackle and no wings—a variety that will often prove very effective when the fish are feeding in that manner. A Marlow Buzz may be included for use on windy days when the larger land insects are blown upon the water.

The flies commonly used by me, with their dressings, are as follows:

WHIRLING DUN (BLUE)

Wings.—Starling or duck, medium light.
Body. —Water-rat or mole fur; two turns of flat gold tinsel around hook at end of body.
Legs. —Glossy ginger or light brown cock's hackle.
Tail. —Three whisks of same.

Pale Evening Dun (Watery Dun)

Wings.—Light starling.
Body. —Lemon mohair lightly dressed.
Legs. —Glossy barred Plymouth Rock cock's hackle.
Tail. —Two or three whisks of same.

Pink Lady

Wings.—Medium starling or duck.
Body. —Pale pink floss ribbed with flat gold tinsel.
Legs. —Ginger or light reddish-brown hackle.
Tail. —Three whisks of same.

Gold-Ribbed Hare's Ear

Wings.—Medium starling or duck.
Body. —Hare's fur ribbed with flat gold tinsel, body not too
    heavy.
Legs. —Hare's fur tied on with silk.
Tail. —Two or three rather long whisks, grey mallard.

Flight's Fancy

Wings.—Light starling or duck.
Body. —Pale yellow floss ribbed with flat gold tinsel.
Legs. —Ginger hackle.
Tail. —Two or three whisks of same.
    The body of this fly will turn green when wet, which is
    nothing against it, however.

Silver Sedge

Wings.—Rather dark starling.
Body. —White floss ribbed with flat silver tinsel.
Legs. —Pale ginger hackle.
Tail. —Two or three whisks of same.
    The body of this fly will turn a greyish-blue when wet,
    but the change does not affect its taking qualities.

WILLOW

Wings.—None.
Body. —Light blue fur, mole or fox, ribbed with light yellow
    silk.
Legs. —Glossy white or transparent hackle.
Tail. —Two whisks of same.

MOLE

Wings.—Medium starling or duck.
Body. —Light mole fur lightly dressed and tightly wound.
Legs. —Purplish-brown (dyed), hackle tied palmer-wise.
Tail. —Three or four whisks of same.
    The standard pattern of this fly is tied with light brown
    woodcock wings.

It is advisable that each of the patterns be tied on hooks
of different sizes—Nos. 10, 12, 14, and 16 will suffice—because the size of the fly is often important, particularly
when the water is very low and clear.

If a greater aid is required in floating the fly (barring the
use of paraffin) other than a stiff hackle at the shoulder,
I would recommend that a short-fibred hackle be tied on at
the shoulder and carried around and down the body to the
tail, the fibres being cut off close to the body after tying.
The effect of this dressing will be to make the fly float
better, particularly after some use, and after the points of
the longer shoulder hackles have been submerged. The
short fibres along the body, by intercepting some light and
permitting some to pass through, will help to produce the
effect of transparency or translucency of the natural insect,
which effect would be particularly noticeable upon flies

where quill is used for the body. The use of this hackle can be dispensed with in the case of those flies where fur or mohair is used for the body, a few fibres picked out with a needle producing much the same appearance and effect.

It may be the experience of other anglers who have experimented with the artificial fly in attempts to produce one that would cock readily and maintain a good balance on the water, that one tied with the wings leaning rather more forward than is the present practice, offers the nearest solution to these difficulties. My own experience is that flies tied in this manner sit beautifully upon the water, but I cannot say that they cock any more frequently than those tied with upright wings. I would suggest that the angler tie a few flies with the wings tilted forward at an angle of about 120°, and try them. If nothing else is accomplished, the experiment may lead to a development in the form of the fly which will enable us all to some day take the one "big fish."

THE SALMON
AND THE DRY FLY

PREFACE

THE experiences which prompted the writing of this little book commenced before the Great War began, and continued until this country entered it.

Having written a book on fly fishing for trout which apparently had met with some little favour, it was suggested that I attempt to present the idea and theories developed by the members of a little coterie of anglers that had been experimenting with the dry fly on large rivers.

Colonel Ambrose Monell, who was responsible in a great measure for the advancement of the art, and who, I believe, was the first angler in this country to take a salmon on a dry fly, was to collaborate with me. Unfortunately, he never saw but part of what is now the first chapter of this book, but I know that he would have agreed with all that has been written. Although it was our intention to confine ourselves entirely to discussing the dry-fly method, it is certain that his great knowledge of this noble fish and his skill with the wet fly would have contributed much to the literature of angling.

The War took him abroad, and, while the work had been started before he left, it was put aside because of more important things. Upon his return it was to be taken up again, but before anything could be done with it he was taken ill and died in May, 1921. Had he survived the War (and he was a casualty just as certainly as if he had been killed on the battle-field), the work would have been worth while.

A better sportsman I have never known. As a salmon angler he was unequalled.

As it is, this meagre book has been prepared by one whose knowledge of and intimacy with the salmon is confined to what might be gained by careful observation in a few years as lives go, but who has been a close student of dry-fly fishing for many.

If these pages interest a few of the many anglers who have been lifelong salmon fishermen, I shall be glad.

Those who may pick up the book to read and scoff at the theories presented are asked to remember that it is intended as a memorial to a man who was a great angler, and if his name is preserved to future generations of sportsmen because of it, I shall be content.

G. M. L. La B.

May, 1924.

CHAPTER I

INTRODUCING A BIG RIVER
TO THE DRY FLY

T HE killing of my first salmon did not in the slightest degree arouse the thrills which, as I have come to know since then, accompany the taking of this splendid fish. It was, perhaps, a stupid fish taken by an even more stupid angler. The rod had been placed in my hands, the place where the fish were lying carefully pointed out, and I had been instructed to take one.

With absolutely no knowledge of the fish I was expected to take and with nothing but ordinary skill in handling a fly rod, my task was difficult enough, and my trepidation was not helping much.

My host, Colonel Ambrose Monell, my companion on many trout-fishing expeditions, had beguiled me with tales of this grand fish into accompanying him to his river, the Upsalquitch, in New Brunswick. I needed but little urging to make the trip and, when I stepped into the river to make my first cast, my only thought was of the manner of handling the vigorous runs and leaps I anticipated that the fish would make. Naturally, I was disappointed when my well-laid plans could not be put into execution. The fly was cast well enough, apparently, to rise a fish, but,

applying trout-stream knowledge to my fishing, and striking as I would have done if trout fishing, I promptly jerked
the fly away from four fish that rose (or perhaps it was one
fish that rose four times) without even pricking a fish. After
being soundly berated by my mentor, I did not strike when
the next rise came, but let the fish set the hook—and was
fast. This fish, although it proved to be but a small one,
felt quite solid, and I prepared myself for a display of the
acrobatic tumbling which had been so vividly described
to me by my angling brethren who knew the salmon. But
never a leap did the salmon make, and I was greatly re-
lieved when the verbal castigation which was being admin-
istered to me was transferred to the fish, which had evidently taken a comfortable position somewhere on the
bottom, prepared to outlast the other end of the line. It
never jumped, it did not make a run; in fact, it did nothing
that a normal, fresh-run salmon is supposed to do. Being
persuaded by the Colonel to force the issue, I exerted
enough pressure on the rod to bring the fish to the surface, eventually towing it ignominiously ashore. My host,
apparently disgusted or exasperated by the exhibition
(mine or the fish's, I did not know which), seized the rod
and determinedly waded into the river. On his second
or third cast he was fast to a much larger fish than the one
I had taken, and, handling it most vigorously, gave a fine
exhibition of what a salmon could be persuaded to do.
As he waded ashore with the fish ready for the net, a
broad smile that illumined his amiable face seemed to me
to say, just as plainly as if he had spoken the words, "I'll
teach the salmon in my river to ridicule me before my

guests." I have not been so sure, since I have had time to reflect over the incident, that he was not really saying to himself, "I'll teach these soft-handed trout fishermen to ridicule the salmon in my river."

Incidents connected with the killing of one's first salmon should and usually do stand out sharply in one's recollection, but in my own case not so brilliantly as to dim the lustre surrounding the taking of many fine fish since which have gloriously upheld the finest traditions of their tribe.

My experience of the next day alone would have driven completely from my mind any lingering doubt I might have had as to the vigour and activity of the salmon. Colonel Monell carried me up the river about five miles, stopping occasionally to fish—he fishing and I watching, which was as I had requested. While the guides were preparing luncheon, at a place which had been purposely selected because of its proximity to a beautiful run that contained many fish and was easily fished, my host persuaded me to take the rod, and directed my operations.

Having by this time learned from observation not to strike when the fish rose, I fastened to a salmon on the first cast, and, as no running fire of caustic comment accompanied the handling of the fish, it is possible that it was killed in a workmanlike manner. At any rate, seven others were laid out on the bank alongside this one before the guide announced that luncheon was ready. Averaging about ten pounds, these beautiful silvery salmon, fresh from the sea, were as strong and as active as any fish I have taken since, leaping frequently and making long runs.

As the fishing was all done on foot and under conditions very similar to those met with on mountain streams, it was like glorified trout fishing to me—except that I was fishing down-stream and with a wet fly.

That evening in camp many things pertaining to fishing were discussed. It rather pleased me to have Colonel Monell concur with me in the belief that the brown trout is a more difficult fish to take than the salmon. As I had had but one day's experience with salmon, I was a little reluctant to express this rather presumptuous opinion, and did so only after he had insisted upon a reply to his question on the subject. He warned me, however, that my experience of the afternoon was unusual and should not be made a basis for fixed opinion. There would be many times, he told me, when, fishing as carefully and skilfully as I might, I should get no fish, although dozens would be visible in the pools. It soon became apparent that the discussion as to the relative merits of the brown trout and the salmon would bring dry-fly fishing into the conversation.

Believing, as I did, that salmon do not feed in fresh water, I hesitated to introduce the subject of fishing for them with a floating fly. Divining, perhaps, what was in my mind, my friend calmly announced that he had killed a fifteen-pound salmon two years before on a dry fly, and assured me that it was not an accident. He had seen the fish rising just as a trout would rise, and, having failed to interest the fish with any of the wet flies in his box, he had deliberately cast across and upstream with a No. 12 Whirling Dun, floating it down over the fish, which took it at once. It was the taking of this fish, and the rising of six

or seven others which he did not hook, that convinced him
it would be possible to kill fish with the dry fly when the
water was low. He would prove to me in the morning, he
said, that fish could be risen to the dry fly—that I would
rise them myself—and he wanted my help in some experiments. I then remembered that at the time the trip was
being planned in town, he had asked me to bring with
me some of the largest dry flies I had, suggesting that
there might be some sea-trout in the river. We did not see
any sea-trout, nor did we look for any. Colonel Monell's
suggestion about the sea-trout was either one of his little
jokes on me, or he was afraid of being considered foolish
on the subject. He really intended that I should use the
dry flies over salmon.

The next morning we sat on the bank of a pool near the
camp and watched the fish—and there were a great many.
Some were in the deep water, some in the shallows at the
tail of the pool; they all seemed listless and apparently
interested in nothing. Suddenly, toward the head of the
pool in rather swift water, I saw a gentle breaking of the
surface, which, had we been on our home waters, would
have been a certain indication that a large trout was feeding. We walked about fifty feet upstream to a point opposite the spot where I had seen the rise, and awaited devel-
opments. In a moment or two we saw a huge snout break
the surface, and then saw the fish sink back about a
foot or so below. We were on the bank, not more than
six feet from this fish, and we watched him for over a half-
hour. He rose regularly and was unmistakably feeding—
or at least taking insects from the surface—for all the world

like a huge trout, rising slowly, pushing his nose above water and quietly taking the insects in. These insects were very small, but we could see them plainly. Nothing in our boxes, however, even approximated them in size, the smallest we had being No. 14 Pale Evening Dun. This was knotted on, and I persuaded Colonel Monell to handle the rod while I observed the actions of the fish. Going downstream thirty or forty feet, he began casting. His first attempt appeared to me to be perfect, the fly alighting apparently directly over the fish, which, instead of taking it, promptly moved about a foot to one side. Fifteen more casts were quite as fruitless. We held a consultation and decided that the failure was due to the size of the fly; and, as we had nothing smaller, we elected to try a larger one, which, after about twenty unavailing casts, was abandoned. Another small Pale Evening Dun was knotted on and another try made. In the mean time, the fish was rising at short intervals, and it was evident that our activities had not disturbed him. The Dun was taken on the second cast and the fish was killed in a few minutes—a beautiful, fourteen-pound, clean fish. It is interesting to note that its mouth and gullet were lined with the small insects it had been taking, but that none were found in the stomach.

The cast which took the fish differed in no way, that I could see at the time, from any of the others which had not been noticed. In the light of later experiences, however, I am convinced that this was one of the most difficult fish we have ever attempted to take with a dry fly. It afforded us an unusual object lesson in the study of stream currents, so important in this method of fishing, which we quite overlooked and neglected, and the advantage we might then have had was lost to us, and was not regained until two years later, when the wider knowledge we had gained on all sorts of water, and the close observance of many fish taken, brought a realization of just how difficult it was to assail the position occupied by this fish.

Anglers who have made a study of dry-fly fishing for trout know how essential it is to study the surface currents of the stream. Knowledge of these surface currents will invariably indicate what is happening below. It is rather a simple matter to illustrate this statement on a stream, and extremely difficult to describe it on paper, but I will attempt it.

A smooth run of water of not greatly varying depth, with only a few small boulders in it, presents rather an easy problem. The flow of water is continuous and is not diverted by obstacles. A fish rising, or seen in a stretch of this sort, is easily cast to, because it remains in the same relative position in which it was first seen. A fly presented anywhere near this position is likely to bring a rise, because the fish is not averse to travelling a short distance for it in water of this character. The glassy, smooth surface in the centre of a deep pool—not the dead water, of course—requires nothing more than skilful, delicate casting over the known or approximate position of the fish, and presents no great problem of surface currents; all other portions of the river do, however, in varying degree, according to the volume of water, the speed of the flow, and its more or less broken surface.

A rising fish may be spotted at the head of a pool, as

was the one we took on the Pale Evening Dun, yet he will not be under the fly when it has been cast to the exact spot where the rise was seen; and this in spite of the fact that the fish has not voluntarily changed his position. This seems rather like a paradox, but it is true, and this is why it is true: to the practised eye, the flow at the head of a pool is seen to be not merely a rush of water into a deeper pocket, but a series of currents of varying speed, each presenting a problem. Close observation of the flattening water just below the turbulent flow will reveal upon the surface numerous wrinkles, or "grooves," as they are termed. Where two currents, flowing at different angles, meet, a well-defined groove will be formed, and this groove will contain more insect food than either of the currents which form it. It is really a sort of eddy, and collects a large portion of the drift stuff which is carried down by both currents. The position of the groove is fixed by the varying pace of the currents which form it. One moment one current will have the mastery, the next it will be pushed back, and, the wrinkle on the surface ever marking the edge of conflict, will move to and fro in a sinuous line. The fish, which is stationed under this groove, is carried back and forth by the converging currents, but is always under the groove, so that a rise in this sort of water, which may have been carefully spotted as being one foot, two feet, or six feet from some point on the shore, would not mean that the fish is where the fly is cast, unless the groove has not changed its course. The fish does not move by any effort of its own; it is merely swung back and forth by the current. This is why the fish which Colonel Monell killed apparently moved away from the fly, when it looked as if it were over him. He was in the groove all of the time, but the fly was not, except at the moment of the cast which took him.

While we were quite well aware of the importance of picking this groove for the placing of the fly on trout streams, we were rather diffident about applying all the rules to a salmon river—the lines of reasoning applicable to the two waters and the two fish being so unlike. I am pleading this as an excuse for not having made the observation at the time Colonel Monell killed his fish. Since then I have applied all the tricks of the trout stream to salmon fishing, with the exception of the imitation of the natural insects, and have found them useful and, in the main, successful.

Of one thing I am certain—in dry-fly fishing for salmon—that, groove or no groove, there are times when the fly must be placed so close to the fish that the distance can be measured by fractions of an inch. This statement must not be construed to mean that the man lives who can cast so accurately that his fly will fall, even once in a dozen casts, at the exact spot, but, as repeated casts properly placed do not seem to alarm the fish, one may hope that at least once in twenty attempts the fly will alight close enough for the fish to take.

The accuracy of one's first cast depends in a great measure upon the distance being covered, and, as it is quite evident that a fly may be cast more accurately to a spot twenty-five feet away than to one fifty feet distant, the angler should get as close to the fish as possible—all things considered.

I could relate many instances where the need for accuracy was so imperative that success was achieved only when the fly was dropped practically on the fish's nose, but I will confine myself to the story of the Forks Pool—and one other.

The Forks Pool is directly in front of the main camp and is formed by the junction of two streams, the Northwest and Southeast Branches of the Upsalquitch River. I doubt if there was a day while the camp was occupied when fish were not taken from this pool. Everybody fished it at some time during the day. There was one small piece that was set apart during our stay for the use of the dry fly only, and I think that the fish taken there on the dry fly were more than half of the number taken from the pool all together. This part was where the Northwest Branch flowed in—a swift, steady current about three feet deep, dropping off into deep water at the edge of the pool. Because of the speed and smooth run of this current, the wrinkles or grooves on the surface were perfectly straight. There were many of these grooves about an inch or two apart, the water between being scarcely ruffled. But on only one of these inch-wide strips of water could the fly be placed with any hope of rising a fish, and one had to know which strip to choose. We could not see the fish, but we knew they were there, because occasionally a snout would be stuck up through the surface, or a fish would leap. This place was fished by Colonel Monell, Beadleston, Hewitt, and myself on so many occasions—one of us handling the rod, with the others looking on offering gratuitous advice—that we came to know, the instant the fly had alighted, whether or not it would induce a rise. There was quite as much sport in watching the other fellow fish as in doing the fishing one's self—and all the while we were learning more and more about our art as it pertained to the salmon in the river.

One day, while watching Beadleston cast all over this water, I remember being fearful that he would rise a fish in some spot other than that one where I felt the fish were lying, and by so doing shatter the theory which had been evolved from our experiences. But after spending a full half-hour at it, he finally killed a large salmon risen on the "sacred inch," and, wading ashore, said, "After that I can be convinced of anything."

We soon learned why this particular groove was productive and the others were not. The fish were lined up along a ledge, and the groove was about four or five inches from its edge. If a fly was cast beyond the groove, the fish did not see it because it was beyond the ledge, while if it was cast too short, they would not move out, fearing, perhaps, that their places in the line would be lost. When a fish was taken, another would move up to the vacant place, and this is why four or five fish could be taken one after the other at short intervals. The fly always had to be placed on the same spot before a rise could be expected, and this certainly proves, I think, that they could not all have been there at the same time. The manner in which the fly was taken indicated, too, that even though a fish might be disposed to take a chance at something near, its desire to retain its position in the line probably controlled its movements and impelled it to refuse to go any distance for the fly.

I have taken many salmon from this ledge, and can recollect only two instances when fish left their positions to take the fly. On each of these occasions, after the fly had floated two or three feet below him, the fish rushed downstream, took it savagely, and immediately turned. Each was firmly hooked, however, and was led to the lower part of the pool. Occasionally a fish would rise smartly, its body beautifully arched as it took the fly on its way down; but more often the rise would be very gentle. Some of these gentle rises would be very exasperating, some of them ludicrous, but they were all very interesting. There was one type of rise where the fish rose lazily and just plucked at the fly, usually missing it completely, in which case it would sink back to its old position as if the affair were of small consequence. Such a fish could be risen a half-dozen times or more before it would be hooked. After the fourth or fifth rise from a fish of this sort, there would be much drying of flies and examination of hook points, following which there might be four or five more rises and misses. Of more determined character, or, perhaps, of more keenness of vision, was the fish which took the fly as a rainbow trout does—rising smoothly, clamping down hard on the fly, and, instead of merely sinking back, diving forward. This chap was usually soundly hooked, and one had to be careful in striking, or find that the fish had kept the fly. Then there were rises by fish that created the impression that they were either nearsighted, or were slow thinkers.

They would rise to a fly where it had been and not where it was; whereupon, finding that it had gone downstream from them, they would fall over backwards with head and shoulders out of the water in their efforts to secure it—which they never did. These fellows sometimes varied the performance, showing that whatever their other infirmities might be, they could maintain an equilibrium. Rising perpendicularly, head and shoulders coming out of the water as before, they would sink back in the same position, for all the world like some stuffed or wooden fish being poked upward at the fly by somebody holding it by the tail underneath the surface.

These incidents were naturally very amusing and entertaining, but could not be considered wholly instructive, because we were dealing with a condition peculiar to this individual piece of water, where what we learned might not be adaptable to other parts of the river unless a like condition prevailed. But the pool really was a fine field for observation, and, because of its productiveness and handiness to the camp, it was frequently fished. Whatever its value may have been to the study of dry-fly fishing in general, certain it is that we learned three things of utmost importance, which, when applied to our fishing along the stream, contributed materially to success, where failure had formerly been our portion.

The first of these was accuracy of casting. While extreme precision was perhaps more essential on water where a fly had to be placed practically on a square inch of surface to induce a rise, the very fact that we were compelled to do so was directly responsible for our effort to cast closer to the fish on the more open water than we had been casting before our study of the Forks Pool. The result was that more fish were risen in other pools and runs than we had ever hoped would be, judging from our former results there.

The second important observation was that a fish was never risen if the fly dragged. Avoiding drag was difficult, but the difficulty was handled satisfactorily by resorting to the old trout-stream method of throwing a loose line. The purpose of a loose line is to permit a fly to travel a greater distance unhampered than it will if the line is cast straight. No sacrifice of accuracy is necessary. The fly is directed to a point a yard or two beyond where it is intended it should fall, and just before delivery is gently pulled back. The result will be that the fly drops properly, but the leader falls in a coil or series of wrinkles upstream, or to the near side of the fish, the effect of which is that the swift water between the angler and the fly does not begin to exert pressure upon the leader until the fly has travelled over the fish. It was difficult to realize that drag, so inimical to success on a trout stream, could have the same effect upon salmon, but it was so. I know from my own experience that, while perhaps a half-dozen or so of grilse have taken the fly when it was dragging, a salmon has rarely done so. Why this is so I cannot say, because sometimes the action of the fly does not appear offensive; but, whatever the cause for the fish's refusal of it, drag must be avoided wherever possible. In my own fishing, where it is not possible to overcome drag, I do not fish with a dry fly.

Another form of drag with which one has to contend in

dry-fly fishing, but which is not quite so disturbing to the fish or irritating to the angler, is what is known as the "retarded drag," which is caused by the leader and line falling on water that is travelling slower than that on which the fly has been placed. The result is that, when the fly is carried downstream to whatever length of loose leader may be with it, it is held back by the rest of the leader and line lying in the slower current. Although this retarded drag is annoying, the fish do not seem to have the same aversion to it as to the other abomination which I have described. Neither of these forms of drag is entirely escapable, but they may be minimized considerably. Calling for a nice calculation, the skilful execution of the cast affords in itself considerable consolation even if a rise is not effected.

The last and perhaps most important observation was that, in our efforts to attain the extreme accuracy apparently so necessary on this run at the head of the Forks Pool, we developed a natural tendency toward dropping the fly very lightly. As the distance being cast was very short—not over twenty-five feet—perfect control of the line was maintained. It was therefore a simple matter not to allow the fly to fall if it appeared to be short, and, if it was overcast, just as easy to draw it gently back while it was still in the air, before permitting it to drop. Alighting practically of its own weight then, as a result of these manœuvres, the fly rested on the water with nothing but the point of the hook underneath the surface, the rest of the fly being above the surface, poised on the hackle points, the body of the fly not touching the water anywhere except, perhaps, at the tail. When the fly was in this position the fish rose to it readily, but rarely was it taken when it was semi-submerged, that is, with the body resting on the surface.

It was the discovery that the fly was ignored by the fish unless it was floating high that prompted the construction of the flies used at the present time. In a great measure, of course, the proper presentation of the fly depends upon the skill of the angler; but as we were not averse to developing, where we could, mechanical aids that might offset errors of casting, we proceeded to build flies that would float high, and discarded many which had been fashioned upon a fallacious principle. For instance, believing that any fly that would float on the surface would perform the function of a dry fly, I spent a great deal of time tying many patterns with cork bodies, on the assumption that in the heavy water of a salmon river cork would be just the thing. It was soon apparent that the heavy body was a detriment rather than an aid, its weight crushing the hackles under it; and, while flies tied in this manner popped up again if they became submerged, they did not take many fish, and were abandoned. Apparently there were no large insects indigenous to these waters, so I was set the task of producing patterns of artificials that would kill.

I hesitate to direct attention to any one of these observations as having a weightier influence upon our conclusions than the others. Inasmuch as the knowledge that fish would rise to a fly which assumed a certain attitude upon the water, and would refuse one that did not, contributed so much to the creation of artificials that would stand up, I am inclined to give first place among our theories to the necessity of having the fly *float high.*

Perhaps the following story of a very successful morning spent on a single pool will best illustrate the necessity, on occasion, of extremely accurate casting, and explain why those of us who use the dry fly firmly believe that a lightly cocked fly, combined with accuracy, is of the utmost importance.

If my recollection serves me, I think that high rod for the first week of our stay recorded seven fish. Our fishing had been done on the lower part of Colonel Monell's water, which ordinarily afforded the best fishing—six to twelve fish per day not being an uncommon take. After all of the pools on this stretch had been thoroughly searched and no fish discovered—here and there perhaps a few grilse —it was obvious that whatever fish had been in this bottom piece had moved upstream. Colonel Monell, determined to ascertain whether or not this conclusion was correct, left that afternoon with his son and Hewitt. Beadleston and I were left to scrape what we could from the almost barren lower water. By diligent and intensive work we each took a brace of fish from Crooked Rapids, a deep pool about five miles down-river from the main camp. On the second day following Colonel Monell's upstream exploration, we were surprised to see a single canoe coming downstream and to recognize the paddler as Colonel Monell's own guide, Murray Everett. Everett told us that there were literally hundreds of fish in the upper pools, particularly those known as Nine Mile and Ten Mile, and that

Mr. Beadleston and myself were to come up immediately, bringing enough food for two or three days. Upon inquiry, we learned that Colonel Monell and Hewitt had had magnificent fishing and were on their way down. Colonel Monell, with the never-failing thoughtfulness and unselfishness which were characteristic of him, had sent for us, not merely to share the fishing with him, because there was not room for four rods, but was abandoning the fishing to us. We met him about halfway between the two camps, and the story he told spurred our guides to such poling as we had rarely seen. We reached camp at dusk with but time enough before dark to kill a grilse for supper. The next day was a red-letter one, if red-letter means something beyond what even a wild imagination would consider a great day. My own fishing resulted in twenty-three salmon and grilse, all killed in one pool before luncheon, and all with a dry fly. Beadleston did not do quite so well on the lower pool, but, after lunching with me as had been arranged, he proceeded to almost even the score, returning most of his fish to the river.

Lest the relating of this take appear to be merely a boastful account of slaughter, let it be remembered that barely enough fish had been killed during the early days of our fishing to supply the table at camp; that not a fish had been shipped to families or friends who were expecting them, and, what was perhaps even more important, the small kegs in which the guides packed the salt fish, upon which they depended to a large extent for their winter food supply, were absolutely empty. These fish were taken for the guides, and when we had enough we stopped, the guides themselves naming the limit. With the exception of two or three, every fish killed was seen before it was cast to. The exceptions were the few grilse which rushed the fly from a distance when it was being offered the larger fish—and they rarely missed it. It was rather exciting, this unlooked-for dash of the grilse. It was also disconcerting, after having cast a yard or so above a large fish, watching intently to observe its action as the fly neared him, to see the fly disappear in a smother of foam as the smaller fish, coming apparently from nowhere, snatched it.

One incident of this sort stands out clearly in my memory, not only because the grilse beat the salmon to the fly, but also because it had a touch that was almost human. About a yard or two from the far side of a salmon lay a grilse—both fish about three feet from the surface. I had cast to the salmon a number of times, being careful not to place the fly too near the grilse, fearing he would take it and disturb the other. It had been near enough, however, for either of the fish to have taken it had one or the other of them so desired, but evidently neither was interested. Finally, the cast which started things was made. As the fly floated down, the salmon started leisurely for it, when, with an amazing dash that carried it over the larger fish, the grilse leaped clear of the water, coming down with mouth open, squarely on the fly, taking it an instant before the big fish reached it. The grilse was quickly subdued and released, and it was my guide, with whom I was discussing the affair, who suggested that neither of them wanted the fly until the other did, when both wanted it, and naturally the quicker one got it. The story would have an added touch of interest, perhaps, if I could go on and tell how I then proceeded to kill the salmon, but the truth is that when the commotion had subsided he was nowhere to be seen.

The pool itself is rather deep and not very large, while the run at the head, which is really part of the pool, is perhaps two hundred feet long and about two to six feet in depth. It was in this stretch that all the fish were killed. With the water as shallow and clear as it was, almost every fish could be plainly seen. Some lay alongside or behind such small boulders as were on the bottom, while others lay quietly in the current. How it was that the fish did not discern our activities on the bank, or, if they did, why they were not disturbed, is difficult to understand, and I am unable to suggest a reasonably satisfactory explanation. Certain it is that the guide and myself were many times within fifteen or twenty feet of a fish to which I was casting, and could observe its every movement. None of these fish seemed interested in the fly at any time except when it was dropped directly in front of them lightly cocked or floating high. When so dropped they would rise leisurely but determinedly, and fasten solidly. No matter how accurate the cast may have been, the fly was utterly refused if even semi-submerged. The conditions under which these fish were taken were ideal. The long stretch of swift shallow water contained a great many fish and was admirably suited to the use of the dry fly.

CHAPTER II
THE DEVELOPMENT OF THE FLY

D
RY-FLY fishing for trout may be briefly described as
that method of angling wherein the angler seeks to
entice and kill the fish by presenting an artificial
fly that is, as nearly as human hands may fashion it, an
exact imitation of the natural insect upon which the fish is
feeding at the time. The theory upon which the system is
based has been demonstrated to be quite sound in principle and practice by its host of devotees. The purpose of
these pages being to relate some experiments and experiences in the use of the dry fly over salmon—a comparatively
new application of the art—a description of the nature and
habits of the salmon, contrasted with those of the trout,
will further that purpose and help the reader to understand why it seems permissible to add to the already volu-
minous literature devoted to fish and fishing.

The trout feeds upon insects that are indigenous to the
stream in which it makes its permanent abode, and is
enticed by an almost exact imitation of its natural food.
Obviously, it is comparatively easy to fashion and present
to a rising trout an imitation, in size and colour at least, of
the particular insect upon which it is feeding. It is even
simpler, perhaps, to present a fair suggestion of some in-

sect to a fish that is not rising, with the hope that it will be taken now and then, and a fair measure of success thus achieved. But the salmon comes into the rivers from the sea to spawn, and is believed not to feed at all while on this errand. The most learned students of the life-habits of this fish are in agreement on this point. It would evidence considerable audacity to ignore the teachings of these authorities, and, so doing, fashion and present to a salmon an imitation of some natural insect, in the hope of exciting his appetite. Imitation of the natural insect, held by many anglers to be the most subtle branch of the art of fly fishing for trout is, therefore, not one of the necessary requirements of the salmon angler, because it would be fruitless to study means of exciting the appetite of a fish that has no appetite to excite. This seemed to me to be so obvious that, when I came to fashion the dry flies that are described later on, no attempt was made to imitate a natural insect, nothwithstanding the fact that I had seen salmon actually taking insects from the surface.

The notion that salmon could be taken on a dry fly appealed to me, and in time became a fixed belief, with the result that I set myself to the task of constructing a series of dry flies which I hoped would successfully demonstrate the correctness of the theory, and thus justify my belief. The great difference between the trout and the salmon in respect to their nature and habits precluded the possibility of applying to the task any special knowledge that had been gained through my experiences on the trout stream, and made it necessary for me to base my experiments upon the habits and peculiarities of the salmon itself, of which I knew very little.

The principles underlying the fashioning and use of the artificial fly as a lure for game fish have been discussed pro and con by theorists for generations. They have not always been in agreement, but their conclusions, speaking generally, are that fish take the artificial fly because they mistake it for food and its presentation excites their hunger, or else they take it because it arouses their anger, resentment, or curiosity. Inasmuch as I was dealing with a fish that does not feed while in fresh water, I had to abandon the hunger theory when I began my experiments in the production of a dry fly, or a series of dry flies, which in form or colour or representation of life could be successfully used over salmon.

Now it is true, perhaps, that salmon may be killed with good imitations of insects, but the efficacy of the cheats can hardly be ascribed to any resemblance they may have to the fish's food, because, as we have seen, the fish does not feed. The most interesting and perhaps the soundest reason advanced in explanation of the taking of the angler's fly or other lure is that, having come into the river to spawn, the salmon resents the intrusion of anything that might disturb its nuptial arrangements, and destroys, or attempts to destroy, the intruder when not too formidable.

It has been suggested that the impulse which prompts the salmon to attack the fly, prawn, spinning minnow, or even the bunch of worms sometimes used successfully in England and in Scotland, is an instinctive provision of nature that impels the salmon to exterminate anything that might endanger the security of the eggs to be spawned, or the safety of the young fish that survive after hatching. The absence of food in the stomach of even fresh-run fish is fairly convincing evidence that none is taken, or at least that none is swallowed. There are persons, however, who contend that emptiness of the alimentary tract does not prove anything; that the salmon does feed, and that the reason why no food is found is because the fish empties its stomach immediately it is hooked or finds itself in a net. Instances have been recorded where small fish and prawns have been found in the stomachs of fish taken, but these instances are so rare that conclusions based upon them are of negligible value. It is conceded that the digestive organs and alimentary canal undergo great contraction while the fish is in the river, due to the enlargement of the procreative organs. This condition undoubtedly prevents the swallowing of such food as might be taken, but cannot be said to desroy the instinct to feed. A fish may take something in its mouth, thereby gratifying a desire to seize its prey, and eject it after a time when it finds it is unable to swallow it.

The salmon must be a gross feeder, when at sea, to acquire the flesh that it does in the short time it is there. It is a wise provision of nature that it does not require sustenance when it comes to fresh water, because otherwise the hordes of salmon which come to the rivers of New Brunswick would fare badly. It is my own belief that salmon do not feed in the rivers, for the reason, perhaps, that they are not moved by hunger to secure food; but it is quite as firmly my belief that the instinct to feed is still strong with them, hence anything that looks eatable is taken. There have been times, it is true, when this theory has been rudely shaken, but another day has usually repaired any damage done it. I have seen many huge fish rising, as regularly as any trout, to minute insects, taking them directly from the surface, which action might indicate that the interest of the fish was aroused by the frequent appearance of these insects on the surface.

Perhaps a little more far-fetched theory is the one suggested by me to some of my friends, to the effect that the fish was reacting to the impulse which prompted vigorous feeding during its earlier life in the river where it was hatched. I should be very proud of this deduction if I could bring myself to believe that either salmon or trout were capable of remembering or discriminating. They are both susceptible to conditions of the moment—the trout particularly—and are deterred from taking the fly because of some unnaturalness, not always apparent to the angler. It may be that the fly has been overcast, which means that the leader, or even the line, is over the fish, or the angler himself has been seen, or his waving rod or his shadow, any one of which will at least distract the attention of the fish from the fly, if it does not actually frighten him.

Here, then, was the foundation upon which a new method of taking salmon was to be erected: the thought foremost in the *trout fisherman's* mind that at least a fair imitation of the fish's food was necessary, coupled with the knowledge that the fish it was hoped could be taken did not feed at all in the rivers. Now, what sort of a fly was it that could be cast upon the surface and interest a fish that had just come from the deep sea? The necessity of having some sort of creation that would float upon turbulent water was obvious, and seemed of most importance. It is difficult enough to float small trout flies on the waters where they belong, and these were all we had with which to begin our experiments with the salmon. On the salmon rivers they remained floating a few seconds at most, and then only when cast with the utmost delicacy and precision upon certain stretches of the stream. The heavier line and leader used with the longer salmon rods tended to drag these small flies under, and it was soon learned that a dragging fly was quite as ineffective as it was on a trout stream.

Overcoming drag was given the greatest consideration, and the conclusion was reached that anything that might be known about the accepted downstream method of wet-fly fishing must be forgotten—except, perhaps, the knowledge of where the fish were lying. The position of the angler with regard to the fish was completely reversed—the fly must be cast upstream, or at best at right angles to the current, and the advantage of covering considerable water with one cast by swinging the fly downstream and across, as with the wet fly, had to be abandoned. As I look back now, faith and hope played prominent parts in the angling that first season. The fly was cast without other design than to have it float. If a fish rose to it—and many did—there was great delight; but if no rise was effected, there were enough reasons to account for the failure. Being obsessed with the idea that not only could salmon be taken on a dry fly, but that more fish could be killed under certain conditions with it than could be killed with a wet fly, failures were accepted with equanimity. The effectiveness of the method was never questioned.

The necessity of fine or accurate imitation being eliminated, I felt the things to be considered could be summarized as follows:

(1) Having a fly that would float high.
(2) Placing fly close to the fish.
(3) Avoiding drag.

It may be safely said, I think, that these are set down here in the order of their importance.

The second and third considerations chiefly concern the angler himself while on the river. No amount of fly-tying will aid a man to place a fly accurately, or to cast it delicately. The remedy is to practise constantly and learn to control as much line as possible; and then, when actually fishing, clean handling of half that length will be a simple matter. Perhaps the best advice I can offer to the salmon angler who is inclined to take this method of fishing seriously, is to accompany some friend or acquaintance, who uses the dry fly, to a near by trout stream on one of his spring excursions. If he has never seen the dry fly fished, the experience will be a revelation to him. Anglers who have adopted this method in their fishing develop a fine skill in the handling of their rods, the accuracy in casting attained by some of them being truly remarkable. They take fish with the floating fly that could not be taken by any other sort of lure. The marked success which attends the use of the dry fly over trout in domestic waters is, in a great measure, responsible for the rapid development of the art on salmon rivers. I may add that one of the great charms of dry-fly fishing—seeing the fly prettily cocked and floating lightly on the surface, the result of delicate and accurate casting—contributed quite as much, perhaps, to the stimulation of our efforts as anything else.

It is quite certain that our experience on trout streams enabled us to take advantage of every opportunity to cheat the obnoxious drag, but in the beginning, handicapped as we were by heavy lines and leaders and small flies, it was discouraging work. We were enabled to meet this difficulty rather less than halfway by the use of some trout leaders, but not much advantage was gained. The stiff rod and the heavy line did not function with the lighter leader, and we were always in danger of losing fish by having the latter break. It was soon apparent that a lighter line and leader were essential and that a rod would have to be built to handle them properly. Colonel Monell undertook to work this problem out, and produced a rod—a two-handed weapon—delightful to handle and quite perfect for the work.

Development of a fly that would float and yet appeal to the fish occupied most of my time and thought during the winter. Ten patterns were created, all of which rose and killed fish the next season; four of them seemed more effective than the others, and after the third season these four patterns, with some important changes, were used exclusively, and now seem to be an adequate variety. Except in size and the extra quantity of hackle which was added to improve their floating qualities, they differed at first but slightly from ordinary trout dry flies. Whatever added buoyancy was gained by the use of the thicker hackles was nullified to some extent by the increased weight of the larger hooks, which were made of rather heavy wire. It was discovered also that the upright wings which had been considered such an important part of the fly absorbed too much water after a few casts to be other than a detriment. I finally decided to abandon the wings entirely and to use hooks of lighter wire. Also, instead of having the hackles tied on at the shoulder alone, I carried them on down the length of the body, palmer-wise. With these changes there was evolved what has since proven to be an almost perfect fly. Encountering, as usual, the difficulty which confronts the dry-fly fisherman in securing hackles of the requisite stiffness, all ideas of creating colour combinations were abandoned in favour of producing flies that would float. Cock's hackles being of finer quality than hen's hackles, they were used exclusively. As dyed feathers were avoided because of an apparent tendency to absorb water, the colours that could be used were limited to the narrow range provided by nature—a few shades of brown and grey. It was fortunate that this was so, because these colours seemed to interest the fish more than the yellows, reds, and blues that·were tried. Possibly the conclusion that the fish preferred some colours to others is not well-founded. That the browns and greys were taken more frequently than the more vivid flies may have been due, of course, to the fact that the anglers themselves had a preference for them and used them oftener. But it is certain that the dyed hackles absorbed water more readily than the natural ones.

The realization that to interest salmon a floating fly had to have a quality which I had ignored, came as a distinct shock. Having spent considerable time in producing patterns with bodies of cork, which were finally abandoned, it was rather disconcerting to learn that the calculation had been made without considering what the fish might think about it. However, the lesson was a valuable one, well worth the time and labour spent on it. The four patterns finally decided upon are the result of five or six years of fly-tying, and experiments on the river. As size is important at times, one may indulge his fancy in this respect to such extent as he pleases, but for all practical purposes sizes from No. 4 to No. 10 will prove quite satisfactory, the intermediate numbers 6 to 8 being best. The use of these sizes will probably excite some comment among anglers who have been accustomed to fishing large flies in heavy waters, but it must be remembered that the dry fly is more frequently used at times when the water is low and probably when wet flies have been of little or no avail. Moreover, while the hooks are small, the flies themselves are large, looking much like pine cones, bottle brushes, and fuzzy caterpillars, and certainly quite unlike anything the fish have ever seen before. Whatever these flies may look like to the fish, the fact remains that they are accepted, and that it is much more important to place them properly on the water than to consider what form or colour they should possess. The list of four follows, and as they are merely adaptations of well-known trout flies, there is

little reason for giving them names other than those by
which they have been known—with one exception, which
is named for the sportsman who contributed so much to
the advancement of the sport, the late Colonel Monell.
This fly was his favourite, as I think it is with all the anglers
who use these patterns. Its dressing, and that of the other
three follows:

COLONEL MONELL

Hackle—Grey Plymouth Rock cock's, tied palmer.
Body —Peacock herl with rib of red, lightly dressed.
Tail   —Five or six whisks of hackle.

SOLDIER PALMER

Hackle—Brown or brownish red, tied palmer.
Body —Red dubbing with rib of tinsel, lightly dressed.
Tail   —Five or six whisks of hackle.

MOLE PALMER

Hackle—Dark brown lightly mixed with grey at shoulder, tied
    palmer.
Body —Brown dubbing or quill, lightly dressed.
Tail   —Five or six whisks of hackle.

PINK LADY PALMER

Hackle—Ginger-coloured, one or two turns of light yellow at
    head, tied palmer.
Body —Light pink silk, rib of gold tinsel, lightly dressed.
Tail   —Five or six whisks of hackle.

I dare not say that one of these patterns is better than
the others, and if I could I would not, for some measure
of satisfaction must be left to the angler who kills a fish

with one pattern after another has been refused—perhaps even one of his own invention.

Much would be taken from the sport if the angler felt that some particular pattern of fly was entirely responsible for his success. Killing a fish with "a something or other," after repeated failures to interest it with well-known or even favourite patterns, is a source of so much gratification, that to destroy it would be shattering one of the chief charms of angling—the secretly cherished belief that a difficult problem has been solved as perhaps no other could have solved it. The angler's confidence in his own perspicacity would in no whit be weakened if it were suggested to him that the "something or other" which took the fish was presented, perhaps, in a more workmanlike or attractive manner. This suggestion would be taken merely as a tribute to his skill.

To the most confirmed believer in the qualities of the Jock Scott or Silver Doctor (I think it is safe to say that these two flies are responsible for more salmon than all other patterns together), a gross of either, no matter how strong one's faith in one or the other might be, would not appear nearly so attractive, nor so complete as a collection, without the addition of some of those patterns which lend colour of their own to a lot of flies, or, because of their dullness, accentuate the brilliance of the two favourites. When experimenting, one may indulge to a vast extent his fancy in colour range, but for all practical purposes I believe the foregoing list will prove satisfactory. It is important that the hackles be stiff; that enough be used to make the finished fly a fluffy thing; and, most important, that the hackle stand out at right angles to the shank of the hook, and all around the body—not merely a mass of fibres on one side and few or none on the other. Even if the fly has less hackle than seems desirable, if what it has stands out straight from the body, it will float higher and last longer than a more heavily dressed fly that mats quickly because it is badly tied. A hackled fly which is not absolutely symmetrical should be shunned if extreme annoyance is to be avoided on the river.

While I am not averse to humouring back into shape a fly which becomes dishevelled after considerable whipping, I detest one that needs attention after every cast. Those so-called "palmers" with the hackles bushy enough, but sloping toward the tail of the fly, should be looked at askance by the angler who wants to float a fly over salmon. When the reader becomes satisfied that a high-riding fly is the first essential to success, he will forgive me for repeating the injunction—*tie the hackle directly at right angles to the body.*

If I had any notion that this book would be taken seriously by salmon anglers, I would like to have that sentence printed in italics at the top of every page. In my opinion, it epitomizes all there is to be said about that part of dry-fly fishing for salmon,—and for trout too,—which is not directly under the control of the angler. If the fly, which is resting on the points of its hackles upon the surface, permits direct rays of light to play upon the under part of the body, and so make it appear more life-like than it would appear if its body were resting directly upon the surface, reflecting no light except that which comes from the water or from the bottom of the river, that, perhaps, is the reason it is more attractive to the fish. But even if that is not really the reason, if we feel that to have the fly float high is essential, what difference does it make? If some day we learn why the fish prefers the fly in one position rather than another, our store of knowledge will be quite complete. On the other hand, if we learn another day that the high-floating fly is ignored, and to be effective the fly must be submerged, where are we? If we could view things as a fish does, or could be sure we know how things look to him, we might get somewhere, but we can't and don't. If we knew everything, where would be the sport, and what would become of all the angler-authors who are destined to write books until the end of time? Personally, I am wedded to the belief that the light which reaches the body of the fly that is *above* the surface of the water really produces an effect more lifelike than any nice discrimination of colour in tying. I have found it absolutely essential on trout streams, and consider this the supreme test. Here, then, is a thought which should appeal to some keen, scientific mind, and I hope it will some day be given the attention I think it deserves.

CHAPTER III

THE GEAR AND SUNDRY OBSERVATIONS

WHILE almost all of my own salmon angling has been done wading, this need not be taken to mean that the tackle suggested is suitable only for this sort of work, or for dry-fly fishing alone. Wherever salmon are fished for with a fly, and whatever method is followed, the rod will be found admirable for the purpose.

The rod, which I will now describe, was designed especially for dry-fly fishing for salmon by the late Colonel Monell, who, besides being an extremely keen and intelligent sportsman, was a trained and skilful analytical engineer. It can hardly be said, then, that it was a chance development, it being reasonable and fair to assume that a really good rod might be the result of intelligent thinking by a man who had both his mind and his heart in his work. This rod, a two-handed weapon, is fourteen feet in length, made in four sections, for ease in transportation. Its weight is about seventeen or eighteen ounces, which would appear at first glance to be inordinately heavy, but as the greater part of this weight (between ten and eleven ounces) is in the butt joint, it will be seen that the rod is not unwieldy. Part of the weight is in a rubber-covered metal button which rests against the body when a fish is on, so the actual

197

weight as indicated by the scales is really deceptive and totally unlike the old "ounce-to-the-foot rod"—not being topheavy and consequently not tiring to use.

It is important to note that one of two qualities should govern one's choice in the selection of any rod—either its suitability for casting the fly well, or for killing the fish easily. If one decides that either of these attributes should be subordinate to the other, he will not be disappointed when he purchases a rod, as it is practically impossible to find a weapon that will fill both requirements mechanically. This is particularly true with respect to fly rods, and especially so if one intends to fish with a dry fly. A dry-fly rod must have power to drive the fly properly, and, with the light leader used in this method of fishing, added stiffness to the rod is certainly of little aid to the angler in driving the hook home, or in handling the fish afterward.

A softer rod which relieves the leader of much of the strain a hooked fish brings to bear upon it will not always cast the fly when and where one wishes to place it. This latter type of rod is a killing rod, and one soon learns that before a fish can be killed it must be risen to the fly and hooked, after which skill in handling will enable the angler to save his fish and tackle, if his paraphernalia be weak in any part. It all depends on whether or not the angler considers it more difficult to kill a fish than to rise it to the fly—or, perhaps, finds more sport in the struggle with the fish after it is hooked than in seeing the fly actually taken when accurately placed. It was Colonel Monell's opinion that rising a fish to the fly, either sunk or floating, was, to use his own words, "eighty per cent of the sport, and killing the fish was any part of the other twenty per cent that the angler chose to allot to it." This statement was made during one of those interminable rides from Montreal to the salmon river, to an elderly angler on the train who had said, during a discussion of methods, that "his guide did the fishing and handed the rod over when he had a fish on." The old gentleman may have meant this in a spirit of banter, but my friend did not permit the opportunity to pass of expressing his opinion upon the subject, and went so far as to say that in his own fishing, after he had hooked a fish, his guide could take the rod if he wished. This, of course, was bending backward a little, because I know that Colonel Monell liked the physical combat. What he really meant was that it took more skill to rise the fish than to kill it—not mere casting ability alone, but knowledge of where the fish should be lying, the size of fly that should be used, and how to swim the fly to it. Unless one is controlled somewhat by this spirit, it will be better for him not to attempt dry-fly fishing. His very impatience to be hung in a fish will defeat his best endeavours.

It is evident, then, that Colonel Monell's rod was primarily a casting rod, but in developing his idea he did not overlook the facts that light leaders (very light ones in comparison to those he had formerly used) had to be utilized, and that some small sacrifice of casting power should be made if the fishing was not to develop into a travesty. By reducing slightly the calibre of the top joint, this concession to the weak leader was made at no great loss to the casting quality of the rod, because a further slight graduation of the next section was made so that a *lighter line* could be used and the balance maintained. The rod will cast a heavy E or light D line perfectly, with the added advantage of having a small-sized line on the water, which will escape much of the drag exerted by the heavy current on lines even one size larger. It embodies nearly everything one could wish for in rod-power adequate to casting a fly as far as one can really fish it, does not require a heavy line to bring out its action or ability to lay a fly lightly upon the water, and last, and least, too, if you agree, has a rather slow action which relieves the leader of a great deal of the strain.

The action of this rod was quite unlike any other that I had used. When I saw the first one, I was skeptical about its quality, but was equally amazed and delighted when I made my first cast with it.

To bring out the best casting quality of this rod, a line of good weight should be used—one that is heavily dressed, but not of large diameter. A tapered line is preferable, but the taper should not be too long if the water being fished is smallish. As the weight of the line beyond the top furnishes the driving power to the fly, it is obvious that a greater length must be used if the line is drawn to a fine taper, or the taper is of considerable length. The long-tapered line would be found to be particularly exasperating in a high wind, and, with a leader of twelve or fourteen feet, almost impossible to handle properly. I am almost tempted to recommend a level line for beginners, and, because of its greater driving power, use one myself quite frequently on blustery days, or when the fly is fished close.

Greater liberties may be taken with salmon than with trout, and, as the short line I fish on the trout stream is a matter of much comment among my friends, this is a rather broad statement; but when I say that I have risen to the fly and killed salmon that were not over twenty feet from me and in plain view all the time I was casting to them, it may not seem so bold. I have taken trout at half that distance, but on a trout stream one may so conceal one's presence that this may be easily accomplished. The trout may be in front of a boulder, or even a smaller stone, and a fly may be placed there from behind, the angler remaining fully hidden. In the larger salmon rivers the fish often lie in water so deep that wading within casting distance is not always feasible. Salmon are less fearful of man, and may be approached with less caution than trout—but not too little. Motion does alarm them, but apparently not to the extent that it does trout. At any rate, if one is careful, a fish may be spotted that is quite close to the angler, and a fair measure of success looked for, if the casting is done quietly and with no undue splashing.

As has been said, if the casts are to be short, the use of a short-tapered or even a level line is recommended. It seems presumptuous to suggest that the line selected should perfectly balance the action of the rod, but I have seen so many badly fitted lines used by men who were otherwise good anglers that I cannot refrain from commenting upon it. If casting the fly is to be a pleasure rather than an effort, close attention must be given to selecting a line that will function with the rod and leader. It is the line which develops the action of the rod, but the sense of power a heavy line gives is the snare in which the angler finds himself enmeshed at times. The line can be too heavy just as it can be too light; so if doubt exists as to the best weight, and there is danger of a mistake being made, try to err on the light side. Lines of the same calibre are not always of the same weight, and the weight of a line is much more important than its diameter. It is quite as important, in dry-fly fishing, that the line be smooth and pliable. A rough line will get rougher, and a hard line is very liable to crack. While this cracking is not likely to impair its strength immediately, it engenders a feeling of insecurity when discovered, and certainly the salmon angler with a big fish on has enough to think of without worrying about whether or not his line is going to stand the strain. The better casting lines are made in lengths of forty yards, which is enough line to permit a reversal of the ends when it is desired. This length, with one hundred yards of six- or nine-thread linen line, well spliced to the casting line, will be more than enough for most rivers. If an undressed silk line is used for backing, it must be watched carefully and dried thoroughly each day, unless it is waterproofed, and even then drying is advised. While some silk lines last well, others fail rapidly. It is a matter of luck if you get a good one, and, as the risk is so great, I suggest a linen line, which I use myself.

The one hundred and forty yards of line should fill the reel comfortably without crowding. For my own fishing, I prefer a single-action, large-spooled reel, with *raised pillars*. Any fly-reel without raised pillars is an abomination. While it is the angler's duty to see that the line is spooled evenly, if, through some chance carelessness, or some abstraction, the line should be piled on one side, the raised pillar will in most cases take care of the excess, while the level pillar, if it does not jam the line and cause a smash with a fish on, will scrape the dressing and ruin it. The click should be extremely light—much lighter than is found on the regulation salmon reel—to prevent too great a strain upon the leader if a fish makes a sudden or determined rush. In fact, the click upon any fly-reel should be just strong enough to prevent overrunning if control of it should be lost for a moment. I cannot bring myself to use a multiplying reel, as my friend Hewitt does, because the outstanding handle is invariably in the way, and a single turn of the loose line, which is always carried in the left hand, around the handle, would end all negotiation with any fish that had taken the fly. The habit of carrying some loose line in one hand while casting will come naturally to the dry-fly angler in time, and should not be considered a wilfully careless or slovenly act. It is essential to shooting the line and dropping the fly lightly. The leader, or gut cast, should be twelve feet in length for the type of rod described. This length will be found to be quite sufficient for all purposes, and if the gut will stand a strain of two and one half pounds dead-weight pull, it will, on this rod, kill any salmon that may be hooked, barring accident. The leaders which were used on the Upsalquitch were made in two sections—one of nine feet, tapered, and one of three feet, level. The latter length was made of the same sized gut as the heavy end of the longer leader to which it was fastened by pulling the two loops together. A spirit of economy prompted this arrangement, as a leader of twelve feet costs about twice as much as one of nine feet. Time was saved, too, because, if the lower length of gut was injured, another nine-foot length was looped on, with the result that one had a brand-new leader of twelve feet. It was found to be much safer to make any necessary change in this way, rather than tie some new gut on the light end of the leader. Knots tied under stress and hurry on the stream were not always as steadfast as those tied at home and at leisure.

When the leaders now used in dry-fly fishing are compared with those which were once used (and still are by some anglers) in wet-fly fishing and which were made of the heaviest gut procurable, it is difficult to believe that the lighter gut will hold fish that occasionally smashed the heavier gut. The heavier the gut, the greater security the angler felt in his fishing, and the cost of these leaders was quite in keeping with this feeling of safety. Ten dollars was not too much to pay for a nine-foot length of this carefully selected gut, while for this sum, or a little more, a dozen of the type used in dry-fly fishing may be procured. They do quite as well also for wet-fly fishing. These price comparisons are not made with intent to influence anglers in favor of the new method on the score of economy. The cost of leaders and flies plays a minor part in the expense of salmon angling, but I venture to say that when one of these favourite leaders parted in a big fish, at some time during the cogitation of the luckless angler the thought that "at the price he should have had the best" intruded itself. No so, however, with the lighter and cheaper gut.

If a smash does come, there are many ways of accounting for it, none of which leaves the angler with much regret. It may be said in this connection that one of these leaders accounted for forty salmon in ten days' fishing without accident, some of the fish weighing up to and over twenty pounds—two very close to this weight being killed in one pool in twenty minutes on the last day. That the finer gut is less likely to be seen by the fish is not the only reason for using it in this style of fishing. The light leaders cause less drag than do the heavier sizes. No reason why they should be used is more important than that.

To illustrate further the real strength of these light leaders and the strain-relieving quality of the Monell rod, among these forty salmon was an eighteen-pound fish that was hooked foul, just behind the dorsal fin, and which was killed after considerable difficulty in eighteen minutes.

I was fishing with a dry fly over the deepest part of the Forks Pool on the Upsalquitch. There were always a large number of fish in this water, and we tried continually to rise one from the middle of it, where it was about fifteen feet in depth. On this occasion, after five or six casts, I had a tremendous rise, and was immediately fast in what seemed the biggest fish ever seen on the river. He would not be budged; sounded almost immediately, and sulked on the bottom. The guides stoned him without effect, and after ten minutes of useless straining, one of the men got into a canoe and tried to move the fish with a pike pole, which manœuvre accomplished its purpose, and the fish ran upstream into the swift water.

I was on foot, and, slowly working my way below him, brought to bear all the pressure that the rod would stand. In a few moments he yielded and started across the pool, at the same time rising to the surface, when it was discovered that he was hooked foul. He swam slowly downstream until he struck the quickening water at the tail of the pool, when he evidently decided to leave the annoying place and go back to the sea. It was impossible to follow very far, as the water was deep and the current very heavy. Just as I was taking to a canoe to follow him, which seemed the logical thing to do, one of the guides, Manzer Giberson, of Plaster Rock, volunteered to net the fish if he could be held a few seconds longer. This was done, not an inch being given against the best efforts of this strong fish swimming with the racing current. The guide waded out considerably above his waist and slid the net under the salmon, bringing it ashore amid the plaudits of his fellow-woodsmen. It was really a dextrous feat for any one to have kept his equilibrium in such water, even unhampered, and this man was over sixty years of age. A better woodsman I have never met. This tale is told, however, to illustrate the remarkable holding power of fine gut when the rod is helping.

It seems hardly fair to tell a story in advocacy of one's pet contention, when there is really another side to it. No one can doubt that a heavier leader would have done as much or even more than did the one used—if the fish could have been risen to the fly with it. Among my possessions is a nine-foot length of the heaviest gut obtainable, which is kept for association's sake and its history. It was used by Colonel Monell in a remarkable manner which not only evidenced its strength, but proved that my friend, while a rare angler, fishing with the finest skill, was moved at times by the primitive instinct which animates us all.

At the run at the upper end of the Forks Pool, which has been described elsewhere, a platform made of a single log had been erected. This log may have been a foot wide —no more, certainly—and it was Colonel Monell's wont to step out to the end of it with a sapling about fifteen feet in length, cut from the forest. To the end of this pole was tied ten feet of line, the famous leader, and a fly. With this outfit Colonel Monell would work the fly back and forth in the current, casting being out of the question, until he hooked a fish. When this occurred, the air was full of fish, imprecations, more fish, jeering suggestions by those on the bank, first to the fish, then to the angler, and finally definite instructions from the angler to his advisers. It was merely a question as to which end of the rod would outlast the other—with the odds better than even on the fish. One may get a fair idea of the power of a twelve-pound salmon by trying this method in some place where conditions will permit; but only good swimmers should attempt it.

My first and only trial resulted in the fish, pole, and outfit being netted a hundred yards downstream, while I was ignominiously being gaffed by our host, near the log. If one had been permitted to follow a fish after hooking it, killing it might have been a simple matter; but the rules laid down by the inventor of this game prohibited one from leaving the log. This particular rule, however, was a poor one. It did not work both ways, as it certainly did not prevent me from leaving the log; however, the relevant point is that the gut outlasted all the smashing attacks upon it.

Any description of dry-fly fishing paraphernalia that did not include mention of at least one of the various preparations for anointing the fly would be incomplete. As an aid to flotation it is quite essential to carry some one of these oils, which are particularly effective on the heavy waters of salmon rivers. The reason for treating the fly with oil is, of course, to cover the feathers and the body so that they will be better able to resist absorption, thus preventing thorough drenching. Dry-fly fishing for trout has become so popular in this country that it is nearly always possible to obtain in any fishing-tackle establishment all of the things that are considered necessary to the method.

Many anglers, even those with a very slight knowledge of chemistry, have endeavored to invent some concoction or decoction that would float the fly under every circumstance, some of them not entirely without success. They have worked upon the theory, and quite correctly, too, that some waxy substance held in solution would produce the desired effect. The most serious difficulty they have met with, however, is in selecting one that would hold the wax or paraffin in solution and remain fluid in the container carried on the stream. This medium should evaporate quickly after the fly has been dressed with it, leaving a coating of the wax on the fibres of the hackles and body of the fly. While in many cases this result is achieved, the stuff is usually so volatile that the angler who puts a bottle of it in his pocket in the morning, containing enough to last through a whole season of fishing, may in the afternoon find traces of it still in his pocket, but none in the bottle. For my own fishing, I am satisfied to use a patented liquid called "Mucilin," the invention of an Englishman, an angling chemist. A single application will keep the fly fairly waterproof for a long time—long enough, in any event, to rise at least one fish. Under the same name is produced a solid substance excellent for use in dressing the line so as to add to its buoyancy.

In "The Dry Fly and Fast Water" I expressed the belief that a floating leader or gut cast was inimical to success in dry-fly fishing, and advised against the use of any substance that would bring the gut too strongly to the notice of the trout. This belief, sound or not as it may be, is the result of an observation made several years ago with a leader floating upon the surface of the water, and the same leader just beneath the surface. The floating gut cast a shadow on the bottom out of all proportion to its diameter, while the shadow of the submerged leader was but slightly distorted. If the leader floating in the depression it made upon the surface obstructed or refracted light to the extent that its shadow on the bottom indicated, a fish midway between it and the bottom would—or shall I say might—be looking, not at a fine bit of gut, but something more like an inch rope. Perhaps this conclusion is not sound, but, whether it is or not, I prefer to have the leader under the surface while fishing, if I can have it there. It is not the simplest thing to do, this casting the fly lightly so that it will drop delicately on its hackle points, and at the same time sink the leader. But, if it is desirable, why use something that will tend to defeat the pur-

pose? One may use the buoyant aid to the line with im-
punity, and with much satisfaction, too; but upon the
leader, never, if there is anything in the foregoing belief.
With twelve feet of gut, or even less than that, between
the fish and the end of the line, the angler need have
no fear of alarming the fish, or even of arousing its
suspicion.

A floating line is more easily picked up from the surface and exerts but a small part of the drag that a sunk
one does. It may travel down-stream more rapidly, but
there is no tendency to pull the fly under. As a matter of
fact, I do not believe that the gut frightens salmon, or
even arouses suspicion in them; but if there is anything in
the idea that the gut floating on the surface is more noticeable than when it is submerged, perhaps the real reason
the fly is refused is because the fish is looking at the gut,
wonderingly, perhaps, his attention being thus distracted
from the fly. I will be so bold as to say that the brown trout
in the streams of New York and Pennsylvania, or anywhere
else, in fact, is a more difficult fish to take than the salmon,
and yet I have had trout rise to the knots in the leader,
totally ignoring the fly. Such an experience invariably has
a chastening effect upon me; and I always wonder what
those British sportsmen—who believe that on much-fished
streams trout become "gut shy" because they have seen it
so often—would say about it. Is this theory of the effect the
sight of the gut has upon fish unsound? Or are they less
particular or more circumspect at one time than another?

Whatever the reason may be for fish rising madly to-day
to any old thing, and to-morrow to nothing, certain it is

that we thrash our brains to a froth hunting it. Getting back to the question of light gut versus coarse gut, shadows of either, floating or submerged, or neither, I think the main endeavour of the angler should be to have the fish see the fly. If its attention is distracted from this important part of the outfit by any of the reasons advanced, why not concentrate on presenting the fly so that it alone will appear to the fish?

It was this thought uppermost in my mind that prompted me to spend so much time in developing a cast that would produce this result, and I may say—with modesty, I hope —that I have, to some extent at least, accomplished its development. I have been criticised because I did not describe it more fully in the book which appeared ten years ago. An understandable explanation of the cast will be a difficult thing for me to make, but, in the hope that many of my angling acquaintances will be mollified, I shall attempt it in another chapter.

CHAPTER IV
CASTING THE CURVE

IT may be justly said, I think, that the literature devoted
to the art of angling for game fish with artificial lures
has been more constructive and helpful during the last
twenty-five years than it was during all of the preceding
years. The tackle used, the rods, reels, lines, gut casts, perhaps most of all, artificial flies, have been so improved that
at this time there seems to be very slight excuse for another
work devoted to the advancement of the art of fly fishing.
Of course,, there will always be differences of opinion as
to the proper method to be pursued in the use of the fly.
New schools of angling—if I may be permitted to use such
a term—will probably arise in the future as they have in
the past. Before the advent of dry-fly fishing the different
schools of trout anglers limited their disputes and discussions almost wholly to the question as to whether
the fly should be fished upstream or down. Later on, the
live question in the minds of those keen for argument, or
with fixed opinions, was: Shall the fly be fished wet or
dry?—a question still open. Controversies concerning the
colour and form of the fly will be with us as long as game
fish inhabit the streams, and are no nearer a satisfactory
settlement now than when they absorbed the interest of

the best angling minds a century or more ago. Until it becomes an established scientific fact that the eye of a fish sees things with the same effect as does the human eye— or what difference, if any, there is between the two in the matter of their observance of an object, with satisfactory explanations made for differences—there will be opportunity for the advocates of colour and the advocates of form to stand about and discourse upon the subject, and support their favourite theory by argument and example.

Notwithstanding the great strides that have been made during the past fifty years in the development of fly fishing, there still remain many problems unsolved, and many things none too satisfactorily explained—the problem of what the fish sees being, perhaps, the foremost.

As far back as 1880, Henry P. Wells experimented with a tank in the back yard of his home in Brooklyn, New York, in an effort to discover if the natural gut cast or leader was less visible than casts coloured or stained various hues. While his method was crude, it proceeded upon the same general principle which has guided the efforts of those who have since made similar attempts.

Perhaps the work of Dr. Francis Ward, "Animal Life Under Water" (1920), gives the best description of what a fly looks like to a trout. His observations were made through a glass window in a chamber set in the bank alongside and below the surface level of a pool. They are of such great value to the angler that I am quoting from his book at considerable length. He says:

"Imagine yourself, then, under the water, on the bed of the river. Seen from below, the surface of the water would appear as an extensive mirror, with the river-bed reflected upon it. Immediately above the observer the reflecting surface is broken by a circular hole or window. Through the surface of the water, in the area of this 'window,' the sky and objects immediately overhead have their usual appearance, but in addition surrounding objects above the water level are also seen through the 'window' as dwarfed and distorted images, suspended, as it were, in the air above the circumference of the circular hole.

"A ring of iridescent colours separates the window from the surrounding reflecting surface." (Henry P. Wells also refers to this iridescence.)

Dr. Ward goes on to say:

"If the observer under the water were to look forward and slightly upward, he would see, on the surface, the arc of his 'window' and an area of total reflection beyond.

"When a fly is thrown over him from behind, he sees: a break in the area of total reflection and a flicker of light as the fly strikes the water. When the fly has settled, only the body, hackle, and hook are visible, with a reflection of the same from the surface. The gut from this point to the edge of the 'window' is difficult to detect. . . . Across the window itself the gut, whatever colour, shows up as a clearly defined dark line."

The photograph which accompanies this description would seem to indicate that the gut was floating, but Dr. Ward does not say so, more's the pity. It would be most interesting if he had described the appearance of the gut both on the surface and sunk. This is the question which is exciting considerable controversy at this time, and one that anglers would like to have answered. Of particular interest to salmon anglers, and of almost equal interest to all fly fishermen, is the following quotation from this charming book:

"My observations of the salmon fly, as it appears when presented to a fish, left me convinced upon one point— viz., that the attraction of the salmon fly lies in the 'flash.' No one can realize the amount of 'flash' from standard patterns until they have seen a 'Jock Scot,' a 'Gordon,' or a 'Doctor' fished past them under water. Colour is, I am sure, an unimportant factor in rendering the salmon fly attractive . . . With our present patterns of flies, changing from one kind to another of exactly the same size, will often result in killing fish; but these changes, when successful, are almost invariably from a quieter to a more gaudy pattern, or the reverse. A glance at a box of salmon flies will show what a change to a more gaudy pattern means— more tinsel on the body, often white eyes on a woodcock wing, and topping tag and hackle made of good reflecting material, all of which points to the fact that it is the increased or diminished amount of 'flash' which gives success.

"The fact that many salmon rivers have their more favoured flies has been advanced in support of the value of colour of different patterns. I go further and say, every pool that has distinctive features—e.g., overhanging rocks or trees, or with flat, low-lying banks—has its more favoured pattern. This is not, however, dependent upon its colour, but upon its light-reflecting power. The 'flash' must be sufficient to attract the fish without causing it to refuse or come short, when it follows the fly.

"In almost every pool there is a particular spot where salmon lie. Not infrequently that spot fishes best from, say, the right-hand bank in the morning and the left-hand in the evening. We can find an explanation for this in the 'flash' of the fly and whether this 'flash' is correctly timed as it passes the fish."

This certainly is an ingenious theory, and perhaps accounts for Hewitt's ability to take salmon on the Upsalquitch pool at 3:20 P.M. and at no other time. I have never gone into the matter quite as deeply as this and really never gave it much thought; but I do know that in trout fishing it has seemed to me that those fish which occupied shaded places were more difficult to take than those which were in the open, without being able to satisfy myself that there was any sound reason for this being so.

The following paragraph, quoted from Dr. Ward's book, must have caused some consternation among the colourists. He says: "Under the water wet flies are seen in two ways. When the fly is well sunk, it is seen against the rocks or vegetation on the bottom, or, at any rate, against the reflecting surface of the water. When fished near the top, it is seen with the bright light of the 'window' as a background. In the former position its killing powers depend upon its form, colour and movement, whereas in the latter position the colour cannot be appreciated."

While this keen observer does not say so specifically, it is a fair assumption from his facts that, if the wet fly just under the surface seen against the bright light of the fish's "window" is not distinguishable as to colour, the dry fly floating upon the surface is just as unrecognizable.

If this is so, the many experiments that have been made in endeavours to throw some light upon the subject have only served to confuse the issue, inasmuch as flies of different colours have assumed neutral shades when viewed through the tanks and boxes used for the purpose, the colours of the flies, though of bright and contrasting hues, proving, in most cases, indistinguishable. Such researches, to be of any value, must be predicated upon the assumed fact that the fish's eye and the human eye are alike in construction and function; and, while the solution of the problem will be of inestimable value to anglers, it seems to me that they must get along without the knowledge until some future investigator solves it for them.

It would appear, then, that anglers who have confined their investigations and experiments to the imitation of insects as they look to them in form and size rather than in colour have accomplished more than those who have attempted to reproduce fine gradations of shade or tint. Whether or not one theory is based upon a sounder foundation than the other is of little importance to the angler at this stage of his interest in the art of dry-fly salmon fishing.

The development of the flies used in dry-fly fishing for trout is perhaps indirectly responsible for the improvement of the form, if not the colour, of flies used in under-water or wet-fly fishing. The wet fly angler could not but admire the beautiful creations which were made by dry-fly enthusiasts to represent the living insects upon which trout feed, and, beholding them, was undoubtedly moved to improve his own lures. The fine discrimination of colour, size, and form of the dry fly probably led to the development of the under-water nymph of Skues and others, and also to the finer art of presentation. Skues, for instance, casts his nymph upstream so that it is suspended just under the surface by the floating leader. His method imitates the swimming larvæ or nymph, or the insect just before the sub-imago stage. In this method of fishing, the wet fly is not moved any more than it is in the dry-fly method. The staunchest adherents to either method must admit that at times the other is more effective than their own; and many anglers are not averse to using either or both when they feel that conditions warrant.

While I never use the wet or sunk fly when trout fishing, it is not because I think that the dry fly will always kill more fish—or even, as some have said, that it is more sportsmanlike—but because it gives me greater pleasure to see the fly actually taken, or to see it floating upon the surface if it is not.

It is a silly notion, perhaps, to go a-fishing and be content not to take fish when they are there to be taken by a man sensible enough to use every sportsmanlike scheme to lure them. I cannot say that I have strictly applied this principle to salmon fishing; although I will state, as an interesting fact in this connection, that during one season I fished the dry fly exclusively—incidentally being high rod for the trip, while I certainly was not the best angler on the river by a wide margin.

Dry-fly fishing for salmon has not reached the point where its devotees may become dogmatic, and, while the floating fly accounted for the most fish at this particular time, it does not necessarily follow that the method proved its superiority over any other. It is more than likely that in my desire to prove something I persevered to a greater extent that did the others, and at any rate it is certain that on one occasion at least, despite the efforts of the most expert wet-fly angler of the lot, the dry fly killed four fish to none, over a stretch of water one hundred yards long. This piece of water was a swift run and always contained fish. It was fished down three times with three sizes of wet flies by Colonel Monell in his best form while I sat on the bank and watched. When he finally admitted that he could not interest the fish, he asked me to try the dry fly over them.

Starting at the bottom of the run and fishing up, the first cast rose a salmon of twelve pounds, which was killed. Before the whole piece had been covered, three more fish were risen, each fish taking with avidity and fastening firmly. It was enough to convince the most skeptical— even the guides, who at first ridiculed the idea, becoming enthusiastic.

When I say the guides ridiculed the method, I mean that they went so far at first as to resent going out with a man who used such silly-looking flies. Afterwards they were moved to such extraordinary efforts in behalf of the angler that one felt that he was imposing on their good nature.

One unforgettable day when Beadleston and I were coming downstream, after a couple of days spent ten miles above the main camp, we elected to fish alternate pools on the way. As we approached the first pool, which

I was to fish, Beadleston, who was in the leading canoe, announced that there was a school of fish along the ledge of rock at the head. My guide beached our canoe gently, and, after waiting about fifteen minutes to let things calm down, I began operations. As the place where the fish were lying had been pointed out to me, and as it seemed also the most likely place for them to be, my first cast was placed where I thought the fish farthest downstream should be resting. There was no response, and, as I worked my fly carefully upstream, covering the likely-looking water, the only interest I aroused was that of a grilse, which smashed the fly hard. I was a bit chagrined, but the guide suggested that the fish were lying below where I had been fishing, and that I should try for them there. This I was loath to do, as their position had been clearly indicated. The ensuing argument was soon settled by the guide, who climbed a tree and located the fish, not below, but about fifty feet above where I had stopped fishing. After telling me that he could see seven fish, and marking them carefully by points on the opposite bank, the guide started to come down. I persuaded him to remain where he was, with the unpremeditated consequence that there was added to the regular and arduous duties of the willing guides on our river the office of "lookout." This meant that, when a piece of water was fished without response, the guide was elected to climb a tree which was high enough to give him a bird's-eye view of the pool, mark down such fish as might be in it, and direct the operations of the angler. This they did willingly, and usually of their own volition. So keen were they for the sport that frequently it was difficult to get them to leave a pool if it contained even a single fish.

To get back to my guide who was left in the tree: I walked up close to where he was perched, and, while lengthening my line straight upstream, questioned him as to distance and the proper angle to be cast. Finally, having a fairly good idea of where the downstream fish was lying, but without being able to see the fish, I cast carefully across to it. My guide announced that I was three feet short and a like distance behind the fish. My next cast was closer, and the third probably dropped the fly over the nose of the fish, for, as soon as it fell, my guide said that it appeared so to him, and in the same breath announced that the fish was coming for it. Simultaneously a huge mouth smashed it, and I was fast in a good one. Again the guide started to clamber down, but being afraid he would not go up again, I bade him remain, and killed the fish unaided. Working the fish downstream, I got the huge net from the canoe and led him into it. This I did with each of the others in turn, taking all but the leader of the school which, naturally, was the largest of the lot. Each time a fish rose to the fly, I was apprised of its coming by the guide, who saw the whole thing, and who was undoubtedly having as much sport as I.

The most interesting part of the whole affair was to hear the guide call out the distance the fly fell from the fish—"three feet," "two feet," or whatever the distance was —and, when he would say, "It is right over him," to wait what seemed to be an interminable length of time, but was really only a fraction of a second, for the ensuing

warning, "He is coming for it," and then to see the huge
fish take the fly. When I had a fish on, my only thought
was to kill it quickly so that I might go back to the next.
I know positively, when it was all over and we stood
admiring the magnificent fish, that my only recollection
was of the six soul-stirring rises. I never saw a man so wildly
enthusiastic as the guide. I had great difficulty in keeping
him on the ground. He wanted to climb every tree that
overhung the stream.

After this experience the same tactics enabled me to take
the next day, among many others, a fish that had withstood
for many days the blandishments of a number of rods,
including my own. This fish lay in the swift tail-run of a
beautiful pool known as "Red Bank." He could be seen
lying in the same position every day, but apparently
could not be moved. The very fact that he could be seen,
I think, was to some extent responsible for our inability
to take him. I mean by this, that, while he was in plain
view, he could not be closely approached because of the
deep and swift current, and long casts had to be made
to reach him. It is my opinion that failure was due entirely
to our miscalculation of distance. While the fly appeared
to be over the fish, probably it never was until at the time
of the cast that succeeded. This was proven when my
guide, who, with the previous day's experience fresh in
his mind, determined to take an observation from a tree
on the opposite bank. When he was firmly ensconced, I
began casting, and threw a long line, dropping the fly—
or so it appeared to me—just over and slightly above the
fish. Imagine my amazement when the voice in the tree

announced that "the fly was eight feet or more short." My casting ability had been strained in making this effort, so, to gain the extra distance, I waded out above my waist and tried again. I was short, but this time only a few feet. A few more tries followed; and then the voice, "Perfect." All this time I could see the fish, and when I was told that the fly was directly over him, it appeared to me to be yards beyond. There was but little time to think of anything else just then, however, as the fish came with a rush, and a few minutes later the breathless guide was netting an eighteen-pound cock fish. This particular fish, however, presented rather an unusual problem, requiring as it did a much longer cast than one would ordinarily be called upon to make. The cast must have been nearer ninety feet than eighty, and anything over seventy feet is difficult while standing in water above one's waist. As a rule, forty feet would be considered a fairly long cast on that stream, and rarely would the angler be called upon to throw farther than that. It is fair to state that ninety per cent of the fish killed were taken at distances under thirty-five feet—in my own fishing, at any rate.

The great distance required to reach this fish, the story of which has just been related, precluded the possibility of throwing the upstream curve in the leader which I invariably attempt in my fishing, and which I will now attempt to describe.

There seems to have been, recently, considerable discussion abroad of the method of making this cast—"curved," I have called it, although Mr. Marston, of the "Fishing Gazette," has dubbed it the "Shepherd's Crook."

It is known on our streams and rivers as the "loop" cast. Whatever name it may finally come to be known by, it is certain that the success which follows its use will make it popular enough with fly fishermen to prompt them to practise it.

Casting a fly is largely a subconscious act. It requires little or no effort except when distance is desired, and no such mental concentration as is required in golf. For the beginner, perhaps, this statement hardly holds true, but it is not my purpose to give instruction to the novice other than to say: watch a good man on the stream; practise; learn to know the action of the rod, and—practise.

Many works on angling include, with great clarity, descriptions of methods of taking fish, the flies to be used under certain and nearly all conditions, the striking or hooking of the fish, and even instructions in handling the fish after it is hooked. The photographs and diagrams in some of these books showing the position a rod should assume, both on the back cast and on the forward cast, are extremely helpful, and an intelligent and earnest reader may learn to correct many bad habits by studying them. It is hoped, however, that the angler interested enough to read these pages, and who may wish to learn the principle of throwing the curved cast by following the none-too-lucid instructions given, will have learned all of these things before making the attempt.

The purpose of the curved cast is obvious. It may be thrown to either the left-hand or right-hand bank, but one is made in an entirely different manner from the other. Both are rather simple, once the principle is understood, and the knack is easily acquired. The execution of these casts will be dependent, to a great extent, upon the familiarity of the angler with his rod—its action, its power, and the "feel" of the line on both forward and back casts. The dry-fly fisherman whose practice has been to "shoot the line," as it is called, knows instinctively when to let his forward cast go so as to have the weight of the live line—that line which is free of the top—pull after it the loose line that is held in his hand. It is this perfect timing that distinguishes the really expert; and, unless one has mastered the rhythm of casting, there is little to be gained in attempting to control the fly after it has been cast.

The cast to the left bank is rather simple of execution, because the angler has control of his line and fly at all times, and, if the fly appears to be going wrong, it may be retrieved before it has touched the water. A false cast or two will generally send it in the right direction, and it may be dropped when the angler is satisfied that it will fall properly.

Assuming that the angler has selected the spot to which he is to direct his fly, his position with respect to his objective should not be at a greater angle than forty-five degrees unless he has attained rare proficiency. Under no circumstances should the attempt be made with more line than can be kept alive in the air without effort and without bungling. A fair length of line to start with would be about thirty-five feet for a two-handed rod of twelve feet or more. Many anglers are prone to use too long a line—an error that is particularly noticeable on our trout streams. It is very gratifying, of course, to lay out a long, beautiful fly, but, as control of the fly is lost after a certain distance is reached, the use of a short line is much more effective where accuracy and delicacy are required. In any event, one must learn to control a short length of line before hoping to attain proficiency with the curve when using the length one has been accustomed to. With thirty-five feet of line that is part of a well-balanced outfit, one should be able to shoot from six to ten feet, or even more, of the loose line held below the hand guide.

The office of the curved cast is twofold on salmon rivers:

(1) To avoid drag.

(2) To keep as much of the leader as possible away from the fish.

On trout streams there is an added advantage which will be considered later, with the hope that the digression may be overlooked.

For the purpose of illustration, let us assume that the angler has taken his position and is about to assail a fish that is visible to him, and which is lying rather close to the bank in open water which has no varying currents. To reach him properly with the fly, one must first judge the distance as accurately as possible. A great aid in ascertaining this is to cast the fly straight upstream, allowing it to fall upon the water at a point assumed to be the correct distance, and, as it alights, to draw an imaginary line on the surface of the water between the fish and the fly. If this results in producing in the mind's eye a triangle in which the fish, the fly, and the angler appear equidistant, the length of line will be found to be quite correct. This sounds rather difficult and geometrical, but if the angler will try it in practice, with a stone or some other object as the other point of the triangle, it will be found rather easy of accomplishment, and very helpful.

Being satisfied as to distance, the angler makes the preliminary dry or false casts toward the fish, but not directly at it. Selecting a spot upon the water about three feet, or even more, upstream from the fish, and using, of live line and line which is held in the hand, about three feet more than it is calculated will reach the fish, the caster should direct the fly to this point, and, as the line is about to straighten, pull or hold back the top of the rod a trifle, just enough to stop the fly in its forward flight. The effect will be to throw the fly out of the direct course it is taking, thus imparting to the line, and obviously to the fly, the impulse to return as it would if being retrieved. If the checking is timed properly, the fly will be thrown downstream, the leader and forward part of the line falling where they are. A sharp curve will be the result, and what has seemed impossible will prove to be very simple. The length and diameter of this curve will be dependent entirely upon the skill of the angler in his timing of the check. Each degree that the rod is held from the vertical will add to the diameter of the curve until the horizontal or side position is reached, when the greatest curve can be thrown. It is advisable, in beginning the attempt, to make this cast from the horizontal position as nearly as is possible. The curve will be more pronounced, and the angler will be less likely to become discouraged. As a matter of fact, those men who are able to throw the curve with the rod held at an angle of less than forty-five degrees from the perpendicular are rarely met. In my own fishing little is achieved from a more acute angle than this. If there is any merit in the belief that the fly alone should be seen by the fish, with this cast the desired result is obtained. If the theory has no merit, the cast is nevertheless worth while, if only because a fly may be so placed that it will float for a comparatively long time before drag is exerted upon it. Particularly is this so on water where a straight cast would be practically useless. It was this consideration that really prompted its development.

In throwing either to a fish that may be seen, or to one that is not visible, but which may be lying in an eddy across a swift current, no change in the principle of the cast is involved. One case, perhaps, calls for a nicer display of accuracy than the other, but that is the only material difference.

There are bits of water on salmon rivers, extremely difficult to fish with a wet fly, that are easily and successfully searched with the dry fly fished in this manner. Those narrow, deep eddies or stickles against a ledge, past which the river races madly, are cases in point. Salmon love to lie in such water, because there they may rest without continuously battling with the swift current. Unless one is very expert, a wet fly rarely reaches these fish, because it is whisked away so rapidly by the pull of the fast water on the line. Downstream fishing does not aid the angler unless a position can be assumed upon the same side of the stream as the eddy. This is not always possible, and, even where it is, a fly is seldom made to swing properly. With the dry fly, however, these places are not difficult problems, because the angler fishes upstream and across. With the fly floating in the eddy, the leader, which is in the current and upstream from the fly, does not exert any drag until the fly has had quite a long drift.

To make this point clearer, let us picture a run such as I have endeavoured to describe where the main current is travelling at, say, three times the speed of that in which the fish are lying, and to which the fly has been cast. If the curved cast is made so that the leader is in the swift water and three feet above the fly, which is in the slower current, the latter will have no pull exerted upon it until the leader has assumed the same curve below it that it had above it. Let us assume, further, for the purpose of illustration, that, if the curve in the leader is a true one (not at all likely, however), it would travel downstream approximately nine feet before it exerted any influence upon the fly if the latter remained stationary—which it does not. This would mean, then, that, while the leader was being carried these nine feet, the fly would have traversed a distance of three feet, entirely unhampered. This would be quite long enough for it to be taken by a fish that was willing, and considerably longer than a wet fly could be induced to remain, unless cast partly upstream by the same method. If the arc formed by the curved leader should have a greater diameter than the three feet used in the calculation, or if the leader were more loosely cast, the fly would naturally ride a longer time in proportionate ratio.

The possibility of some obstacle preventing the proper handling of one's rod to throw the curve suggests the "loosely cast" leader. Where exigency forces the cast to be made with the rod in a position perpendicular to the river, the loose cast is very effective on water where drag must be overcome. It is particularly effective where the fish cannot be reached from below and where the fly must be drifted down from above. The loose cast is accomplished by casting in the ordinary overhead manner, with more line than is required to reach the objective, drawing the fly back sharply just before it alights upon the water. This action causes the leader to fall in rather ragged shape, and is not over-pretty, but, until its convolutions are straightened out by the current, the fly is not greatly interfered with. The time given the fish with this cast is but a fraction of that afforded him by the curved cast, but certainly this short time is better than none. It is most effective when fished across and a trifle downstream, the angler endeavouring to have the fly fall below the leader or downstream from it. Notwithstanding its rather messy look on the water, the tortuous leader will often reward the angler when other methods fail.

This cast is mentioned because of its great value under certain circumstances and conditions. When they prevail and it is advisable for the angler to use the cast, it will be well to remember that the fly should not be placed as far in an eddy as it is with the curved, horizontal cast. Observing this injunction, he will be surprised to see how long his fly will remain afloat close to the edge of the swift water, and how frequently it will be taken. It is essential to observe also that, while the fly is primarily being directed toward a certain spot on the surface of the water, it should be cast as if the real objective were a point in the air about five feet above the surface and a like distance beyond the spot intended to be reached. When the line is straight and the check applied, the whole affair will drop lightly on the water, the fly coming back to the desired point, and I really think that the cast is more difficult of accomplishment than the curved one, calling as it does for a nicer calculation of distance.

Attempting to describe how this or that cast should be made all seems so useless, when one is really unable to analyse and describe his own handling of rod and line so that it may be put in writing that will be intelligible. On the river it is a very simple matter to illustrate and explain the reason for anything that is done by giving a practical demonstration, and a keen observer will often detect little things that are helpful to him which may have escaped the notice of the demonstrator himself. It is all very much like the advice of the expert fly-tier, who gives lucid printed instructions for tying this fly or that, but forgets, or is unable, to describe the little touch given here and there which makes his own creations perfect specimens, while the fly tied by another, according to his formula, is an awful thing to contemplate. I know, because I have tied flies by rote—with a pattern on the table to copy. It just can't be done.

In handling a rod on the stream, nearly every motion is instinctive. A certain sharp turn of the hand to give decisiveness to a cut in cheating the wind on a rough day, or a slight upward flicking of the line before actually retrieving the fly, which aids in lifting it from the water with little or no disturbance, are actions that are individual and that do not lend themselves readily to description. There are many other helpful little tricks easily learned, but not so easily taught—by means of the printed page, at any rate. Having prepared my excuse in advance for what the reader may consider a dismal attempt to describe another cast—and the only other I shall attempt to describe—attention is called to the fact that the description of the curved cast already given dealt only with throwing the fly to the left-hand bank, looking upstream, by a right-handed angler. It is obvious that unless the angler be ambidextrous or casts exceptionally well from over the left shoulder with the rod held in the right hand, the same cast to the right-hand bank is practically impossible. Even with a single-handed rod this over-the-shoulder cast is difficult and not nearly so neat in execution. With a two-handed rod it is almost useless to attempt it. The long two-handed rod and the longer line used on salmon rivers are most unwieldy when anything beyond direct casting is necessary. By shifting hands on the butt of the rod, one is enabled at times to throw a slight curve to the opposite bank, but the result is not apt to be very successful or satisfactory. The position is an unnatural one, and because of this the cast is usually a bungle. Nevertheless, whether or not one is skilful in handling the rod in this manner, the curve may be thrown in another manner without any feeling of awkwardness.

It has been pointed out that, in throwing the left curve, constant and perfect control of the line must be maintained. This control is a simple matter, because, if the fly appears to be about to fall improperly, it may be retrieved and the false or air casts continued until the caster is satisfied that its direction is approximately correct. Not so, however, with the curve to the right, because to execute it correctly the angler must deliberately *lose control* of the line. When neatly done, this abandonment of the fly when it is but halfway on its errand is, in my opinion, the most effective cast made with a fly rod, and is extremely fascinating to watch. Its purpose, of course, is to cheat the current as long as possible of the abominable drag.

The length of time a fly can be induced to remain in the slower current is amazing, due entirely to the fact that a much larger and more effective curve may be thrown to the right than to the left. There is the added advantage that the curve to the right may be thrown from almost any angle—almost directly upstream, in fact—and the angler is then less likely to be seen by the fish on the narrow parts of the river. This cast calls for nothing more than the ordinary manner of handling the rod, except at the moment of the actual delivery of the fly. No extraordinary effort is called for beyond a certain nicety in timing. It may be made with the rod held in any position from the vertical to the horizontal, the exigency of the occasion only governing the choice of attitude. The usual false or air casts for measuring distance and direction may be made, but a much longer line than is indicated by the position of the point being assailed must be used. The exact amount of loose line to be held in the hand will be learned when the angler has made two or three successful attempts.

The greater the distance the fly is to be cast, the more loose line must be held in the left hand. No hard-and-fast

rule may be set down for this, but when the angler has
learned just what his rod will do, the quantity required
will also be known, instinctively. I have said that the usual
false or air casts may be made and should be made with
no deviation from the usual form except in one respect.
While keeping the line alive in the air, the water to be
fished should be carefully scrutinized, and the fly in its forward flight should bisect an imaginary line drawn at right
angles from the bank to a point in the stream, about eight
or ten feet (according to the length of the leader) from
where the fly is to be dropped. At the moment it is decided
to release the fly, it is helpful to imagine that the casting
line has *neither fly nor leader attached to it*. With this
thought in mind, the cast is then delivered as if the object
was to drop the *end of the line* at the point where the
imaginary line on the surface has been bisected.

When it is determined that the line, in the preliminary
casts, is over this point and the final fishing cast is to be
made, instead of permitting the live line to exert its fullest
energy upon the line held in the hand, which results in
what is called "shooting," this energy is deliberately killed
by prematurely releasing the line that is held. This action
results in depriving the forward part of the line and leader
of life, the energy which would have been imparted to
them, had the line been held, being destroyed. In other
words, the impulse which has been given the line, and
which would have travelled its whole length to the fly, is
now diverted to pulling out the loose line. This line and
that part free of the top which is exerting the pull will use
up all of the energy, and the line beyond that point will

die and fall where it is. This means that, if the release is timed correctly, the energy fails when the line is still in the looped position it assumes in the ordinary forward cast before the line has straightened out. It is really nothing more or less than an incomplete straight cast, but if these directions are correctly followed, the line may be made to fall on the water as gently as in any other cast. The line drops first almost to its end, the leader and fly falling afterward, but at a considerable distance from, and at a right angle to, the end of the line, usually in a more delicate manner than if the straight cast had been made. The curve described is greater in scope, and hence more effective, than the left-hand curve, and I think it is almost as easily executed.

I have never been able to view this cast except from behind the rod, and consequently am unable to describe accurately just what action the fly takes at the moment it is about to alight. Discussing it recently with some of my angling friends, and desiring to get their ideas, I was given six different opinions, none of them satisfactory. One—and not the least observant of them—insisted that the line travelled straight to its full length and then the leader and fly turned in toward the bank directly at a right angle. This, of course, is impossible, but with the idea in mind this man practised one whole summer, and, naturally, became hopelessly confused. He was put upon the right track and was delighted to find he could do it easily. Another of these gentlemen averred that the fly was propelled toward the bank by a secondary motion of the rod—also impracticable. He was guided gently in the right direction also. They

were unanimous, however, in declaring that the line falling
first upon the water did not mar in the slightest degree the
effect of the fall of the fly. On the contrary, they maintained that the fly could not be placed quite so delicately
in any other manner.

The reason for the fly alighting more delicately when
thrown with the curve is easily explained. While a fly
thrown perfectly straight can be made to drop softly, it is
obvious that, when line and leader are suspended for an
instant in the air and then begin to fall, the fly partakes to
some extent of the weight of the line and leader and falls
more rapidly than if dropping merely of its own weight.

With the curved cast, the line falls on the water first,
and the fly, instead of dropping steadily from the time it
begins to fall, rises again in the air, usually when it is
about a foot from the water, and then falls, with nothing
to accelerate its descent but a foot or two of gut. It may,
and frequently does, touch the water lightly some distance
from the objective point, when it is again lifted by the
leader which is still travelling slowly forward and dropped
with a skipping action a yard or more away. When this
occurs, the fly rises about a foot or two in the air, so that
its actual fall is from this distance.

Nearly all salmon fishermen are trout fishermen too, or
were, or will be; so for the benefit of even a single individual who may be a trout-stream angler and is interested,
I must call attention to the value of this right-hand curve in
fishing the fly for trout in runs or stickles under overhanging bushes.

Frequently the best water in a run will be close to the

bank; in many cases it will be completely covered by alder branches, rhododendrons, and the like. Such places invariably hold trout, and very good fish as a rule; but with only two or three inches of space between the branches and the water, it is practically impossible to cast a fly underneath them far enough to interest one. If the caster is expert, or perhaps fortunate, the fly may occasionally be shot in, but it is usually quickly pulled out by the leader as the current drags it downstream.

Desirable above all else in these places is the floating of a fly well under this tangle for a yard or two. With the right curve this may be accomplished. Usually there will be found along the bank an opening in the bushes which may not be over a foot or so wide. This space will be quite enough, and a fly placed there will drift down under the branches for a long distance. There is, of course, the danger of hanging up on some unseen under-water thing, but it· is amazing how often the fly will clear such obstructions. Even if one does get hung, there is a measure of satisfaction in having the fly in this difficult water, if but for a moment; and certainly the danger of fastening on some trash under the branches is not so great as that courted by attempts to place the fly just along the edge of the bushes by direct casting.

Another source of satisfaction is the feeling that such places are only for the man who can fish them properly. The ability to control the fly in this sort of water will mean to the clever angler some good sport on hot summer days when there is none to be had on other parts of the stream. I hope the development and practice of the cast will not depopulate our trout streams. One thing is certain, however; anglers who master it—and they will be many—will use it constantly on all parts of the river after they come to realize its effectiveness—overhanging bushes or no bushes.

On many of our smaller streams there are some extremely fruitful bits of smooth, rapid water completely overhung by alders, on which the orthodox overhead cast is useless and often impossible. The trout in these runs are rarely taken, except occasionally by downstream wet-fly anglers or bait fishermen. The upstream wet-fly or dry-fly man may sometimes be able to fish certain parts of the lower reach of these stretches, but always feels that the most productive water has to be abandoned because of his inability to place a fly on it. If he is a master of the side or horizontal cast, he will reach farther upstream than the average angler, but will even then have difficulty in placing his fly, except in one general direction. Particularly effective on water of this character is the right-hand curve. Using the short, eight-foot rod, so much the vogue among dry-fly men at this time, the advantage it gives over even a nine-foot rod is considerable.

If the caster will back up solidly against the left-hand bank, practically burying himself in the alder or willow branches, and face directly across the stream, the horizontal cast, in combination with the curve, will enable him to cover almost every bit of water available to the fly. It will be of advantage to the angler fishing this water to note that the distance travelled by the tip of his rod must be confined to a very small arc. If the rod is stopped in its forward motion at a right angle to the stream, there will be little or no danger of hanging up, either behind or in front. Standing in this position also affords a view of the back cast which under such conditions requires almost as much attention as the forward cast.

All of these instructions and admonitions are predicated, of course, upon the assumption that the angler is master of his rod, or at least knows the importance of a well-balanced outfit. In this connection let me say again that I believe a level line, or at least one with a short taper, will accomplish more than the finely tapered affair usually selected by the dry-fly man. These long tapered lines are wonderful for attaining distance combined with delicacy, but for the smaller streams and for this cast the short tapered line is preferable.

For the benefit of anglers who are not entirely familiar with the trick of casting a long line and a delicately dropped fly, known as "shooting" the line I will endeavour to explain further. A properly functioning rod, line, and leader are absolutely essential before the cast can be discussed or understood. These the angler must provide for himself, and in the following explanation it is assumed that he has already done so.

As we are dealing primarily with salmon fishing, and although the same principle is applied to trout fishing with the dainty eight-foot rod of three and one half ounces, we will use the fourteen-foot rod in the illustration. Starting with nothing but the leader of twelve feet free of the top, an attempt to cast the fly is made. How far may it be thrown? Irrespective of the actual twelve feet of gut one has for casting, is it a simple matter to throw the fly even this distance? Of course one may reach the fly out to a point equal to the length of the rod, plus a portion of the length of the leader, but he will be fortunate if, in his attempt, the whole outfit does not slip back through the guides until the fly is found resting snugly in the top guide, pulled there by the weight of the line, which runs along the rod from reel to tip. Adding a few feet of line from the top to the leader, a bit more control is secured, but not much. Again it may slide back. This proves that force may not be applied to the fly itself with any hope of result. An additional twenty feet of line, however, will give the caster a feeling of control, and the fly may be neatly cast; but still the proper sensation of power is lacking.

With forty feet of line out, a radical change in the "feel" of the rod takes place. It is as if the fly had suddenly acquired weight, and the caster begins to feel that something solid is actually being thrown. The action and power of the rod are now brought into being, because the free line has actual weight, and this weight is exerting its influence. As the line is lengthened, its weight increases, and it is the utilization of just the proper measure that the rod will stand without losing power that determines the amount of line that may be extended. I detest mathematical calculations in connection with my fishing, and personally believe that they teach us little about a rod (one usually selects the rod that suits his own hand), but a few figures here may help a clumsy explanation. The line which has been found most suitable for the fourteen-foot rod is level, forty yards long, and weighs one ounce, eleven drams. If forty feet of this line is used in our experimental cast, there will be a weight of nine drams, to which energy is imparted and which will exert its influence on the rod.

Let us assume that this length of line has been cast and is lying at full length on the surface of the water in front of the angler, about to be retrieved, preparatory to another forward cast. As the lines goes back of the rod, it travels in the form (theoretically) of a semi-ellipse, the proportions of which are assumed to be perfect when the fly is directly over the top of the rod. If the rod is stopped in its backward motion, and no other force is applied to it, the line, when its energy is expended, should fall back of the angler in relatively the same position it occupied when it was in front of him. We are not concerned with this stage of the cast, however, but are intent upon bringing the line forward again. When the fly has reached a certain point behind the angler (not considered here mathematically), the entire weight of the line, plus the force which has been imparted to it will be felt, this being the signal for beginning the forward cast. The same force is again applied, the line, leader, and fly travelling—or should be travelling—in the same elliptical curve as they did on the retrieve. It is this part of the cast with which we are deeply concerned, and it deserves considerable study. The pull which was felt, and which indicated that it was time to begin the forward cast, is felt again after the rod has been stopped; this is the signal for releasing the line held in the hand, the resultant carrying out of this line by the live line being termed "shooting." It should be evident, then—or I have not made myself clear—that the energy which carries out the loose line would have been exerted elsewhere if this line were held tightly. "Elsewhere" means along the live line until it reached the fly, which, if this were permitted, would either fall heavily, or be jerked back by the heavier and now inert line. The "shoot" prevents this, and the fly will travel on gently, being impelled by only part of the energy which started the cast, the rest being exhausted in carrying out the heavier line below the top of the rod—that part which has been held in the hand in readiness for the pull. Let us study this a bit further. The energy which has been transmitted to the line has come from the forward and downward push on the rod—this energy travelling up the rod from the hand to the line, and along the line to the fly. As soon as the line has been started in its forward movement, the impulse it has received must expend itself. This it does by seeking the point of least resistance—in our case, the fly on the end of the leader. As the line assumes its curved position, which it does as soon as the impulse is applied, the energy which impels its forward motion is confined to the "belly" of the line. The "belly" of the line, so-called, is that part which is in the form of a semi-circle or half-curve—the lower part of which is held tightly by the top of the rod, the upper portion being that part of the line to which the leader is attached. The "belly" is now in a vertical position, with the line below and above it occupying relatively the same planes.

At some point in its forward flight the energy confined to this "belly" exerts its strongest influence upon the flight of the fly. Where this point is, the angler must discover for himself, as it is impossible to fix a distance by any mathe-

matical calculation except for each individual rod. Let us
suppose, however, that we are using forty feet of line
which has weight and a leader of twelve feet, the weight
of which is negligible. When the fly in its forward flight is
directly over the top of the rod, there would be fifty-two
feet of live line and leader in front of the rod. If this line
and leader assume the form of the theoretical semi-ellipse,
the length of the under part of the line would be, let us
say, twenty-six feet, not allowing for the curve. The upper
part would also be twenty-six feet long, but would be part
leader, making the proper proportions of the heavier line
twenty-six feet below and fourteen feet above. The
twenty-six feet below, however, would now be without
energy, the balance of which, after being used to extend
these twenty-six feet, is now being exerted upon the upper
fourteen feet and the leader. What is the result? The fly,
which has followed the direction of the line practically in
the same plane, is thrown forward until line and leader
form a straight line (again theoretically). As the line behind the leader is now inert, it begins to fall to the water,
and as its weight is greater than that of the leader, it falls
more rapidly. In its fall it forms a curve, and, as the line is
no longer straight, the result is that the fly is pulled back,
and does not fall upon the water fifty-two feet distant. This
effect may be exaggerated in one way or another, depending entirely upon the force applied to the rod. If the impulse given the line is too great for its length, the farther
back will the fly be jerked. If the force applied be too
slight, the line will not carry the fly to even its own length.
Hence, I say that the angler must be guided by his own

judgment in applying the proper force and in determining when the line is exerting its greatest energy before he can hope to time the shooting of it correctly. Having done this, he will discover that when ten feet of the loose line is carried out, the energy which accomplished this has been taken from another part of the line—that is, the leader. He will also learn that the leader and fly are still under the forward impulse, and are not retarded by an inert line, but are connected with a line that is travelling in the same direction, and which is still going forward, under the influence of the force which has been divided. It is this correct timing that will lay out line, leader, and fly in almost perfect alignment, so that the whole affair will fall practically at the same time, and very delicately.

Having acquired this knowledge, the angler is ready to try the right-hand curve, the purpose of which is, of course, to *prevent* that straightening of line and leader which naturally results in an attempt to destroy, in part, the energy which has been imparted to them. This energy is not permitted to travel down to the fly, but merely to carry it along for a certain distance and to a certain point. In other words, the fly never quite catches up with the line, but when it is dropped, falls in a plane parallel with and about opposite to the other end of the leader, or behind it. The distance the fly falls away from the rest of the line will depend, in great measure, upon the style of cast used. The horizontal or side cast will produce the largest curve, as the line is travelling in the proper plane and is in the position in which it should fall upon the water. If a vertical cast is necessary, a satisfactory curve may be thrown by deflecting the point of the rod toward the objective at the time the forward impetus is given, and a rather sharp downward cut made to the right. This particular vertical cut probably requires a bit more finesse than the horizontal cast, calling, as it does, for a preliminary estimate of the effect that the change in the plane the fly follows from the back cast to a new forward one will have upon the result. It is not difficult, however, and the fly is easily controlled.

While the curved casts which I have attempted to describe are the results of observation made while dry-fly fishing, and are recommended primarily for use in this method of fishing, there is no good reason for their not being used when the wet fly is being fished. In many places on the river, while wet-fly fishing, I have resorted to one or the other of these casts when it was difficult to swim a fly to a fish downstream—usually with success. That they are considered of importance on both salmon rivers and trout streams is evidenced by the number of anglers who use them at the present time.

On one occasion, while demonstrating the right-hand curve to a friend, the cast met with a surprising result. The river was abnormally low; so low, in fact, that at this point we were compelled to wade the shallow water, while the guides pulled the canoes upstream. When the stream was normal, this stretch was a heavy rapid, but at this time there were only a few pockets here and there against the bank, while the middle of the river was not quite a foot deep. We toiled laboriously for a hundred yards over the rough bottom and through the water, which, while shallow, was swift enough. Near the top of this stretch we

found one of these pockets about ten feet long and not
over six feet wide lying snugly against the undermined
bank. On a trout stream it would have been an ideal spot
for a big fish, and it was this thought that prompted my
companion to suggest that it was just the place for a practical illustration of the effectiveness of the curved cast. It
was a difficult spot to reach because of the boulders that
lay between us and the pool. The current in the pocket
was rather swift, and a fairly large curve had to be thrown
if the fly was to remain upon the surface for even a short
time. However, I approached the pocket boldly, explaining, as I did so, just where the fly should be placed and
how it should act after it had alighted. Fortunately, everything went well, and, while pointing out to my friend and
the guides the different speeds of the surface currents as
indicated by the action of the leader and the fly, we were
dumbfounded to see the fly disappear in a terrific swirl, as
a huge fish rose to it. He did not fasten, however, and as I
retrieved my fly, trying to think of something to say, I
found that my friend was even more inarticulate. Finally,
recovering his composure, he said that the demonstration
was conclusive, but that I must take the fish so that he
could believe what he thought he had seen. It was incredible, in his opinion, that a fish could be occupying such a
cubby-hole, and he was determined to see what sort of
thing it was. Giving no thought in my excitement to anything but the desire to rise the fish again, I let myself in
for a very bad ten minutes. Again the fly was cast in almost
the same spot, and again came the fierce dash—and this
time there was no miss. The fish was solidly hung, and, as

he felt the barb, made a prodigious leap. While I looked about wildly for the easiest line of retreat, I had no idea of what the fish might do, but he evidently had planned a campaign in the event of just such an attack. It did not take him over ten seconds to decide that a haven could be found downstream, and out he came and down he went, with everybody following as best he could over the slippery stones, while I gave line when I could not keep up. Finally the fish was killed in the pool at the bottom of the run, but I feel certain that had I been compelled to follow him twenty yards farther over the rough bottom, the story would have to be told without giving the weight of the fish, which was sixteen pounds. This was the reddest fish I have ever taken; apparently he had been in the river a long time and probably had ensconced himself in the place when the water was high, determined to remain there until his wedding day.

The surprising result of the demonstration did not prove so much the efficacy of the curved cast as it did that fish may frequently be found in curious places. The taking of this fish was undoubtedly responsible for much wasted effort on the part of my friend and myself in fishing many similar corners which probably contained no fish. However this may be, I feel certain that the fish could not have been taken on any cast other than a curved one—certainly not with a dry fly.

The switch cast is used by many anglers to reach places and to overcome obstacles such as I have described, but, while their dexterity enables them to place a fly where they wish, it is usually delivered with a comparatively straight line, and its effect can in no way be compared with that achieved by the curved cast. Usually the switch cast is resorted to when there is difficulty behind the angler, and in this respect it is an invaluable aid; but even when well executed, it is a messy and noisy affair, certainly not to be recommended as preferable to the other casts mentioned. There are times when it must be used or any hope of having the fly on the water has to be abandoned, and I think it quite within the ability of some men to throw a curve with it. If this can be done, it might be well for those skilful enough to execute it to add it to their accomplishments. I have not tried it myself, because my attempts at switch casting have aroused in me no very keen measure of satisfaction, which may account for my prejudice against it.

Perhaps, in a book like this, made up as it is, in the greater part, of observations on dry-fly fishing, a description of the manner in which a curved cast should be fished out may not be out of place. All trout fishermen know, of course, that, after the dry fly has been placed upon the surface of the stream, it is not moved in any way by any impulse from the rod. The trout fisherman refrains from moving his fly, because doing so destroys the imitation he has been trying to create—that of a natural, unhampered insect drifting with the current. In salmon fishing, any action imparted to the fly is apparently just as detrimental; not for the same reasons, but because the effect produced is very similar to that which is exerted by drag, which seems very offensive to the fish.

The angler who attempts for the first time either of the curved casts, particularly that to the right-hand bank, which is hardly more difficult than the one to the left, will probably be slightly embarrassed when he finds that a greater length of loose line than he is accustomed to handling lies between his rod and the fly. His first thought will be concerned with the control of this unusual amount of slack line in the event of a rise. He ought not to be unduly perturbed if he will follow this direction: as soon as the fly alights, the rod should be held in a horizontal position pointing directly at the fly, and should be kept in this position for as long as the fly is floating naturally. As the fly drifts downstream, the line will become even more slack, which slack should be taken up by stripping in the line with the left hand. The rod may be held in the right hand alone, by resting the butt against the body, thus leaving the left hand free to handle the line. When the rise comes, by allowing some of the loose line to pass back through the guides, the rod may be raised to the vertical—the correct position as the hook is pressed home. The action of stripping in the line should be free and determined—a foot or two at a time—not to the point of pulling or jerking, however—so as to keep pace with the fly. Line recovered during this process should be held in loose coils in the hand that gathers it, where it is read for the next forward cast. If this appears to be too hazardous a procedure, the line may be slowly reeled in. Should no rise be effected, the line which has been gathered will have shortened the casting line to such an extent that lifting it from the water preparatory to another cast will be acomplished without difficulty.

No attempt at retrieving the fly should be made before it is opposite or even below the angler, or until it is no longer floating straight downstream, but is beginning to swing across the current under the influence of the dragging leader. When drag begins, the efficacy of that particular cast has ended, and the angler should give his immediate attention to retrieving the fly before it may be drawn under the surface and become thoroughly drenched. Considerable annoyance will be avoided if the fly is retrieved at the right moment; it should not be permitted to drag downstream until the line is straight. Many anglers have allowed themselves to fall into this bad habit, probably with the idea in mind that the stretched-out line is more easily controlled. Their reasoning is logical, but not sufficiently comprehensive. Perfect control may also be maintained if the line is stripped in rapidly up to the point where the fly is opposite the angler. The retrieve may then be made with little disturbance of the water and little or no danger of submerging the fly. Once the fly has gone completely under the water, it is no longer the fluffy thing that had been cast upon the surface, even though it may have been well treated with the best moisture-repelling substance. Should the fly, unhappily, become drenched, its restorative treatment consists merely of pressing it firmly between the folds of a handkerchief—a bandanna by preference. A smart rap or two against the waders or coatsleeve before squeeezing (if the latter be point-proof) will relieve the fly of most of the water, leaving the bandanna in better condition for the next drying. Four or five short, sharp air casts should whip the fly quite dry, ready for another cast. If, however, after this handling, the fly sags on its hackles as soon as it alights, it should be retired temporarily and a new fly used. The discarded fly may be stuck somewhere—in the hat, preferably—and after an hour or two's exposure to the sun should be in condition to be used again. It should receive another application of the Mucilin just before it is cast.

Palmer flies such as those used for this sort of fishing are rather sturdy things, and more liberties may be taken with them than with the more delicate, winged patterns when they need humouring back into shape. Pulling the fly through the fingers from tail to head will cause the hackles to stand out at right angles to the body again, when through much whipping or wetting they tend to slope toward the tail. If, after these ministrations, the fly refuses to sit up, it should be discarded at once, for that day at least. No amount of fly dressing will add to its buoyancy, once the hackles become sodden and soft. A thorough drying is the only remedy.

A description of the life and habits of the fish we are pursuing, together, perhaps, with a short history of the lives of the insects which are indigenous to the rivers he frequents, and the manner in which rods are made and flies are tied, might properly be considered to come within the scope of a work of this sort. These things, however, are known to the writer in a perfunctory way only, and, instead of making scientific researches, time was devoted to developing his fishing along what might be called grosser lines.

The knowledge that some form of imitation is necessary, where artificial lures are used, prompted the thought that a fair representation of the *action* of the natural insect while it was on the water was perhaps more important and might prove more effective than following closely its colour or form. This belief resulted in most attention being given to the proper handling of rod and line which would enable the angler best to simulate this action. This does not mean that manipulation of the fly after it has been cast is necessary, or was even given a thought. On the contrary, when the artificial fly assumed the passive attitude of the natural insect as it rests upon the surface, it was then believed to be imitating its action best. This really means that the fly is to be dropped lightly, is to rest upon the surface on the hackle points only, and drift downstream unhampered by the gut cast or leader. In the effort to produce what was considered the necessary effect, there was developed what is known as the "curved cast," the cast which I have just attempted to describe. These observations were made upon trout streams where the course is very difficult and their application to salmon rivers has proved quite as satisfactory.

If any skill in this direction has been developed, or if any refinement entered into the experiment, the determination to master the rod is alone responsible. This attitude toward the sport is unquestionably a selfish one, and perhaps there is not much justification for putting into print thoughts on the subject prompted by such a motive.

However this may be, if these few pages arouse the interest of some real angler-author and induce him to explain intelligently how the angler should comport himself and his rod while on the stream, they will not have been in vain.